W9-AAB-715

Protect, Clean Up and Speed Up Your Computer for Seniors

Studio Visual Steps

Protect, Clean Up and Speed Up Your Computer for Seniors

Use the protection, clean up and optimization tools available in Windows

www.visualsteps.com

MOHAWK VALLEY
LIBRARY SYSTEM
CENTRAL BOOK AID

This book has been written using the Visual Steps™ method.
Cover design by Studio Willemien Haagsma bNO

© 2011 Visual Steps
Edited by Jolanda Ligthart, Rilana Groot and Mara Kok
Translated by Chris Hollingsworth, *1ˢᵗ Resources* and Irene Venditti, *i-write* translation services.

First printing: September 2011
ISBN 978 90 5905 257 4

All rights reserved. No part of this publication may be reproduced, stored in a retrieval system or transmitted in any form or by any means, electronic, mechanical, photocopying, recording, scanning or otherwise, except as permitted under Sections 107 or 108 of the 1976 United States Copyright Act, without the prior written permission of the Publisher.

LIMIT OF LIABILITY/DISCLAIMER OF WARRANTY: While the publisher and author have used their best efforts in preparing this book, they make no representations or warranties with respect to the accuracy or completeness of the contents of this book and specifically disclaim any implied warranties of merchantability or fitness for a particular purpose. No warranty may be created or extended by sales representatives or written sales materials. The advice and strategies contained herein may not be suitable for your situation. You should consult with a professional where appropriate. Neither the publisher nor author shall be liable for any loss of profit or any other commercial damages, including but not limited to special, incidental, consequential or other damages.

Trademarks: Visual Steps is a trademark of Visual Steps B.V. in the Netherlands. Windows is a registered trademark or trademark of Microsoft Corporation in the United States and/or other countries. All other trademarks are the property of their respective owners.

Resources used: Some of the computer terms and definitions seen here in this book have been taken from descriptions found online at the Windows Help and Support website.

Do you have questions or suggestions?
E-mail: info@visualsteps.com

Would you like more information?
www.visualsteps.com

Website for this book:
www.visualsteps.com/protect
Here you can register your book.

Register your book
We will keep you aware of any important changes that are necessary to you as a user of the book. You can also take advantage of our periodic newsletter informing you of our product releases, company news, tips & tricks, special offers, free guides, etcetera.

Table of Contents

Foreword

Dear readers,

In this book we will explain step by step how to safely use *Windows* to protect and clean up your computer and improve its overall performance. You will learn how to protect your computer from viruses and spyware and how to adjust the security settings in *Internet Explorer*.
By using *Disk Defragmenter*, among others, and by managing the autorun programs, you can improve your computer's performance significantly. You can also use *Disk Analyzer* to check for errors on your hard drive.
You will find that *Windows* runs faster and is more stable, once you have thoroughly cleaned up your computer!

I wish you lots of success with this book!

Alex Wit
Studio Visual Steps

P.S. We welcome all comments and suggestions regarding this book.
Our e-mail address is: info@visualsteps.com

Visual Steps Newsletter

All Visual Steps books follow the same methodology: clear and concise step-by-step instructions with screen shots to demonstrate each task. A complete list of all our books can be found on our website **www.visualsteps.com** You can also sign up to receive our **free Visual Steps Newsletter**.
In this Newsletter you will receive periodic information by e-mail regarding:
- the latest titles and previously released books;
- special offers, supplemental chapters, tips and free informative booklets.
Also, our Newsletter subscribers may download any of the documents listed on the web pages **www.visualsteps.com/info_downloads** and **www.visualsteps.com/tips**
When you subscribe to our Newsletter you can be assured that we will never use your e-mail address for any purpose other than sending you the information as previously described. We will not share this address with any third-party. Each Newsletter also contains a one-click link to unsubscribe.

Introduction to Visual Steps™

The Visual Steps handbooks and manuals are the best instructional materials available for learning how to work with computers and computer programs. Nowhere else will you find better support for getting to know the computer, the Internet, *Windows* or related software.

Properties of the Visual Steps books:
- **Comprehensible contents**
  Addresses the needs of the beginner or intermediate computer user for a manual written in simple, straight-forward English.
- **Clear structure**
  Precise, easy to follow instructions. The material is broken down into small enough segments to allow for easy absorption.
- **Screen shots of every step**
  Quickly compare what you see on your own computer screen with the screen shots in the book. Pointers and tips guide you when new windows are opened so you always know what to do next.
- **Get started right away**
  All you have to do is switch on your computer, place the book next to your keyboard, and begin at once.

In short, I believe these manuals will be excellent guides for you.
dr. H. van der Meij

Faculty of Applied Education, Department of Instruction Technology, University of Twente, the Netherlands

Register Your Book

When you can register your book, you will be kept informed of any important changes that are necessary to you as a user of the book. You can also take advantage of our periodic Newsletter informing you of our product releases, company news, tips & tricks, special offers, etc.

What You Will Need

In order to work through this book, you will need a number of things on your computer:

Your computer should run the English version of **Windows 7, Windows Vista** or **Windows XP**.

Network and Internet
View network status and tasks
Choose homegroup and sharing options

In order to download *Microsoft Security Essentials* you will need an active Internet connection.

How to Use This Book

This book has been written using the Visual Steps™ method. You can work through this book independently at your own pace.

In this Visual Steps™ book, you will see various icons. This is what they mean:

Techniques
These icons indicate an action to be carried out:

⊕ The mouse icon means you should do something with the mouse.

▦ The keyboard icon means you should type something on the keyboard.

☞ The hand icon means you should do something else, for example insert a CD-ROM in the computer. It is also used to remind you of something you have learned before.

In addition to these icons, in some areas of this book *extra assistance* is provided to help you successfully work through each chapter.

Help
These icons indicate that extra help is available:

 The arrow icon warns you about something.

 The bandage icon will help you if something has gone wrong.

1 Have you forgotten how to do something? The number next to the footsteps tells you where to look it up at the end of the book in the appendix *How Do I Do That Again?*

In separate boxes you will find tips or additional, background information.

Extra information
Information boxes are denoted by these icons:

📖 The book icon gives you extra background information that you can read at your convenience. This extra information is not necessary for working through the book.

 The light bulb icon indicates an extra tip for using the program.

Prior Computer Experience

If you want to use this book, you will need some basic computer skills. If you do not have these skills, it is a good idea to read one of the following books first:

Windows 7 for SENIORS - ISBN 978 90 5905 126 3
Windows Vista for SENIORS - ISBN 978 90 5905 274 1
Windows XP for SENIORS - ISBN 978 90 5905 044 0

Test Your Knowledge

Have you finished reading this book? Then test your knowledge with a test. Visit the website: **www.ccforseniors.com**

This multiple-choice test will tell you how good your computer knowledge is. If you pass the test, you will receive your free *Computer Certificate* by e-mail.

Website

On the website that accompanies this book, **www.visualsteps.com/protect**, you will find further information. This website will also keep you informed of any errata, recent updates or other changes you need to be aware of, as a user of the book. Don't forget to visit our website **www.visualsteps.com** from time to time to read about new books and other useful information such as handy computer tips, frequently asked questions and informative booklets.

For Teachers

This book is designed as a self-study guide. It is also well suited for use in a group or a classroom setting. For this purpose, we offer a free teacher's manual containing information about how to prepare for the course (including didactic teaching methods) and testing materials. You can download this teacher's manual (PDF file) from the website which accompanies this book: **www.visualsteps.com/protect**

The Screen Shots

The screen shots in this book were made on a computer running *Windows 7 Ultimate* edition. The screen shots used in this book indicate which button, folder, file or hyperlink you need to click on your computer screen. In the instruction text (in **bold** letters) you will see a small image of the item you need to click. The black line will point you to the right place on your screen.
The small screen shots that are printed in this book are not meant to be completely legible all the time. This is not necessary, as you will see these images on your own computer screen in real size and fully legible.

Here you see an example of an instruction text and a screen shot. The black line indicates where to find this item on your own computer screen:

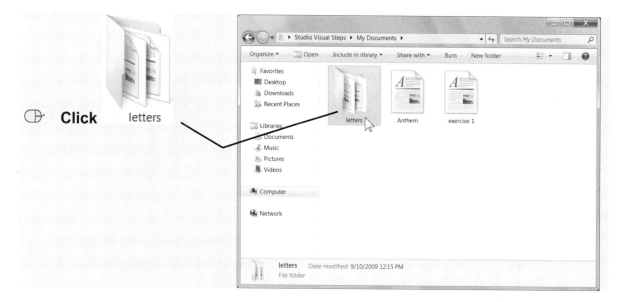

Sometimes the screen shot shows only a portion of a window. Here is an example:

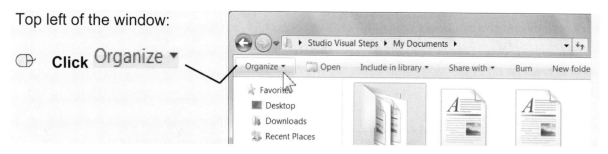

It really will **not be necessary** for you to read all the information in the screen shots in this book. Always use the screen shots in combination with the image you see on your own computer screen.

1. Security

Security is crucial if you connect your computer to the Internet. An adequate security system will reduce the risk of contracting *viruses* and prevent harmful software from being installed onto your computer. A virus is a program that attempts to spread from one computer to another causing damage to the computer (by deleting or damaging data), or by simply being a nuisance (by displaying unwanted messages or changing the information that is displayed on the screen).
A computer that is contaminated by viruses can cause a lot of irritation. It will not only annoy you, but may also annoy other people as well. If your computer contains a virus, it can also contaminate other computers. You may not notice this, because it can happen while you are sending an e-mail message, or a chat message. Or if you are sharing files from a CD, DVD, Blu-ray disk, or a USB stick. As a computer user you are responsible for your own computer's security. To protect your computer, you can use a *firewall* and an updated *antivirus program*. You should also make sure that your computer is regularly scanned for viruses or other harmful software.
Windows offers a useful security tool: the *Action Center* (*Windows 7*) or the *Security Center* (*Windows Vista* and *Windows XP*). You can use this tool to check your computer's security settings for *Windows* and modify them, if necessary.
In order to be protected from viruses and unwanted software, such as spyware, you will need to install an antivirus program. *Microsoft Security Essentials* is just one of the many antivirus programs that are available today. In this chapter you will learn how to download and install the free *Microsoft Security Essentials* program.
In the last part of this chapter we will explain how to safeguard your privacy and how to use the Internet in a more secure manner when using programs such as *Internet Explorer*, *Windows Live Mail* or *Outlook Express*.

In this chapter you will learn how to:

- use the *Action Center* or the *Security Center*;
- set up a firewall;
- download and install *Microsoft Security Essentials*;
- scan for viruses;
- change the settings for *Microsoft Security Essentials*;
- modify the security and privacy settings in *Internet Explorer*;
- prevent phishing;
- set the *SmartScreen* filter;
- set the pop-up blocker;
- manage add-ons;
- filter unwanted e-mail messages.

➥ Please note:

To perform the actions described in this chapter, you will need to use the administrator's account (be logged in as administrator). If you cannot use this account, you will not be able to change several settings. When this happens, *Windows* will display a warning message. In such a case you can just read through the relevant section.

➥ Please note:

The screen shots in this chapter have been made in *Internet Explorer 9*. If any of the operations are different in *Internet Explorer 8*, they will also be explained.

➥ Please note:

In several sections, various *Windows* editions will be discussed simultaneously. This means the screen shots in this book may differ from what you actually see on your own computer.

1.1 The Action Center in Windows 7

The *Windows 7 Action Center* checks the security settings for your computer and installs the automatic *Windows* updates, provided you have enabled the *Automatic Updating* function. In the *Action Center* you can also check your computer's maintenance status and update it as needed as well as solve various other computer problems.

This is how you open the *Action Center*:

☞ **Click**  ,

☞ **Click** System and Security

☞ **Click** Action Center

In the *Action Center* you can view the status of the main components of your computer's security system, such as:

- *Firewall*
- *Automatic updates*
- *Protection from unwanted software*
- *Other security settings*

You will be able to see at a glance if there are any problems occurring on your computer and what these problems are about. The problems will be indicated by a red or yellow color. A red color indicates a major problem which will need to be solved as soon as possible, for instance installing new antivirus software. A yellow color indicates a maintenance task that you might need to perform, such as scanning the computer for spyware.

Please note: your computer's settings may differ from the settings in this example.

☞ **Close the *Action Center* ⚆²**

Tip

View problems on the taskbar

In *Windows 7*, you can check the taskbar for maintenance or security problems on your computer:

To the right of the taskbar you will see an icon with a flag

and a red cross 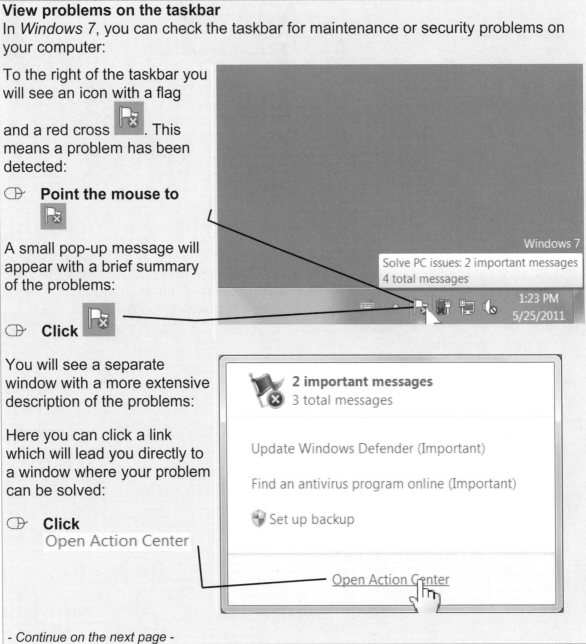. This means a problem has been detected:

☞ **Point the mouse to**

A small pop-up message will appear with a brief summary of the problems:

☞ **Click**

You will see a separate window with a more extensive description of the problems:

Here you can click a link which will lead you directly to a window where your problem can be solved:

☞ **Click**
   Open Action Center

Windows 7

Solve PC issues: 2 important messages
4 total messages

1:23 PM
5/25/2011

2 important messages
3 total messages

Update Windows Defender (Important)

Find an antivirus program online (Important)

Set up backup

Open Action Center

- Continue on the next page -

Now you will see the *Action Center*:

Possible problems will be displayed: ————

You will also see some extra options for solving the problems: —

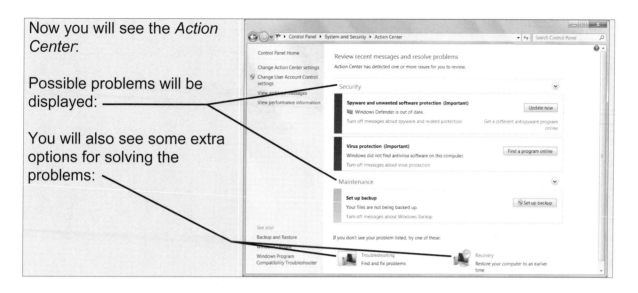

1.2 The Security Center in Windows Vista

The *Windows Vista Security Center* checks the security settings for your computer and installs the automatic *Windows* updates provided you have enabled the *Automatic Updating* function.

This is how you open the *Security Center*:

☞ **Click** , **Control Panel**

☞ **Click** Security

☞ **Click** Security Center

☞ **If necessary, give permission to continue**

In the *Security Center* you
can view the status of the
main components of your
computer's security system,
such as:

- *Firewall*
- *Automatic updates*
- *Protection from unwanted
  software*
- *Other security settings*

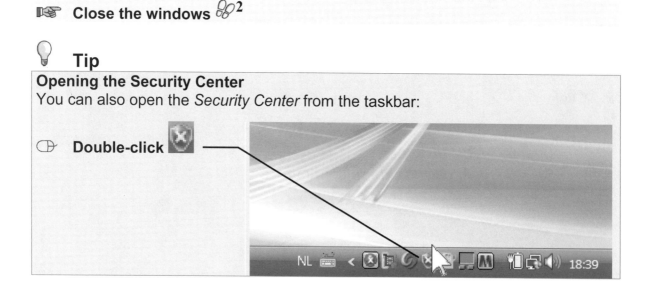

You will be able to see at a glance if there are any current computer problems. The
problems are indicated by a red color. A red color means that the problem needs to
be solved as soon as possible, for instance, by installing antivirus software.

Please note: your computer's settings may differ from the settings in this example.

☞ **Close the windows** 🐾²

💡 **Tip**

Opening the Security Center
You can also open the *Security Center* from the taskbar:

👆 **Double-click**

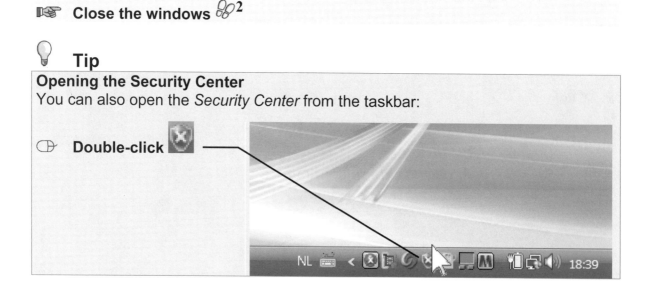

1.3 The Security Center in Windows XP

The *Windows XP Security Center* checks your computer's security settings and installs the automatic *Windows* updates provided you have enabled the *Automatic Updating* function.

This is how you open the *Security Center*:

☞ **Click** start , Control Panel

☞ **Click** Security Center

In the *Security Center* you can view the status of the main components of your computer's security system:

• *Firewall*
• *Automatic updates*
• *Other security settings*

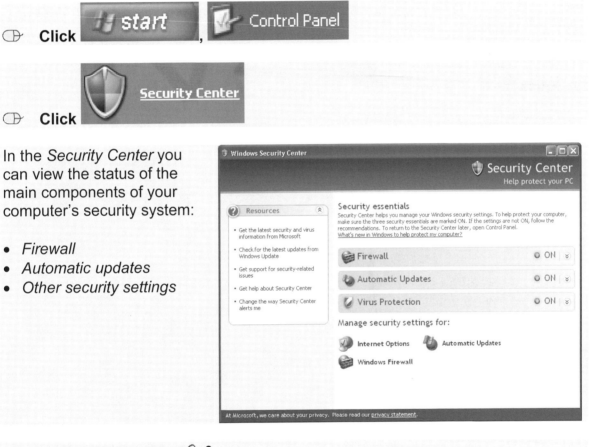

☞ **Close the windows** 👣²

1.4 Setting Up the Windows Firewall in Windows 7

A *firewall* is a software or hardware component that regulates the ingoing and outgoing data traffic between your computer and the Internet and/or other networks. Depending on your firewall's settings, traffic is either blocked or allowed.

The word 'firewall' sounds a lot safer than it is. A firewall will not protect your computer from viruses. If the firewall allows your e-mail program to connect to the Internet, it is still possible to receive an e-mail message containing an attachment with a virus in it. The firewall does not check the contents of the data traffic.

☞ **Click**

☞ **Click** System and Security

☞ **Click** Windows Firewall

The green icon 🛡 indicates that the *Windows Firewall* has been enabled: ─────────

You may have a different firewall installed on your computer. In that case you will need to disable *Windows Firewall* by clicking the Turn Windows Firewall on or off link: ─────────

Using two different firewalls at once will cause system conflicts.

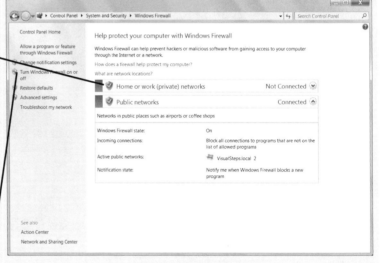

You can also change the *Windows Firewall* settings:

☞ **Click**
Change notification settings

You will see the *Customize settings* window:

You can enable a firewall for various network types:

Block all programs, for instance for a public wireless network:

Display a message for each new program:

Usually, the default settings will suffice.

☞ **Click** Cancel

If you are using a program that needs to receive data from the Internet or from a network, the firewall will ask you to allow the connection. You can modify the settings in this window:

☞ **Click**
Allow a program or feature through Windows Firewall

For each connection that is allowed, an exception will be added to this list:

You can use the Change settings button,

and then the Allow another program... button, to directly add programs:

For now, you will not need to change these settings:

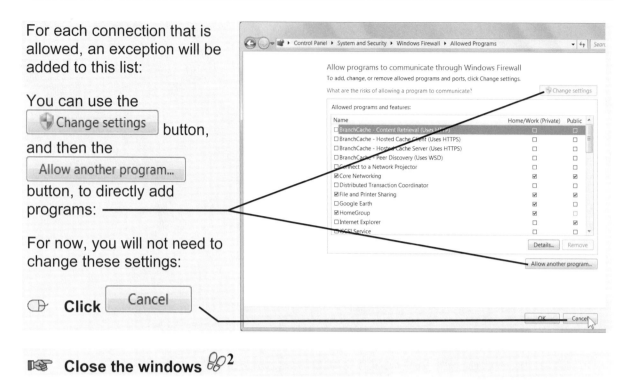

👉 **Click** Cancel

👉 **Close the windows** 👣²

1.5 Setting Up the Windows Firewall in Windows Vista

A *firewall* is a software or hardware component that regulates the ingoing and outgoing data traffic between your computer and the Internet and/or other networks. Depending on your firewall's settings, traffic is either blocked or allowed.

The word 'firewall' sounds a lot safer than it is. A firewall will not protect your computer from viruses. If the firewall allows your e-mail program to connect to the Internet, it is still possible to receive an e-mail message containing an attachment with a virus in it. The firewall does not check the contents of the data traffic.

👉 **Click** , Control Panel

👉 **Click** Security

👉 **Click** Windows Firewall

You will see the *Windows Firewall* window:

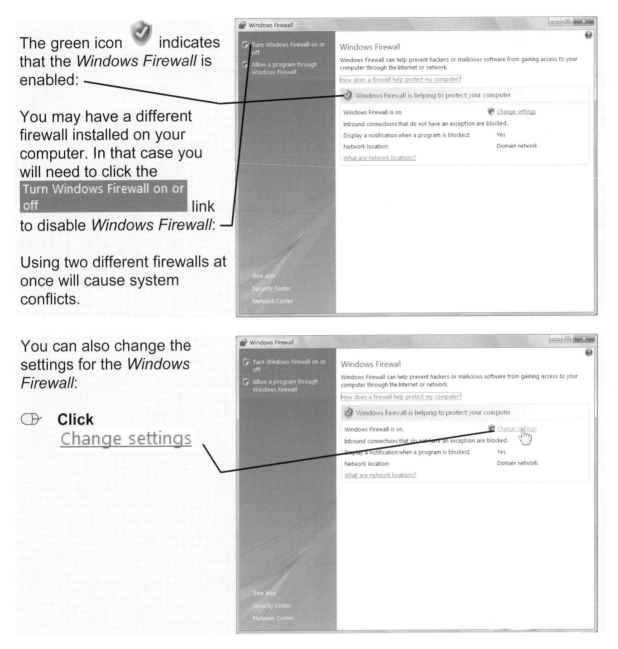

The green icon indicates that the *Windows Firewall* is enabled:

You may have a different firewall installed on your computer. In that case you will need to click the Turn Windows Firewall on or off link to disable *Windows Firewall*:

Using two different firewalls at once will cause system conflicts.

You can also change the settings for the *Windows Firewall*:

☞ **Click**

Change settings

☞ **If necessary, give permission to continue**

You will see the *Windows Firewall Settings* window:

Block all programs, except the programs you want to allow: ─────

Block all programs, for instance, in a public network:

Disable the firewall: ─────

⟳ **Click** [Cancel]

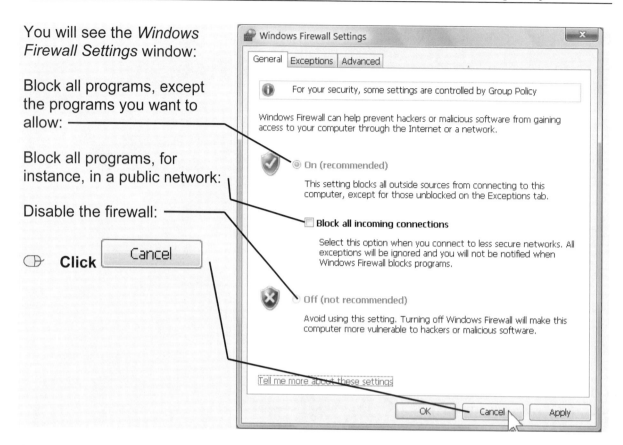

If you are using a program that needs to receive data from the Internet or from a network, you can tell the firewall to make an exception. You can do this in the window below:

⟳ **Click**
Allow a program through Windows Firewall

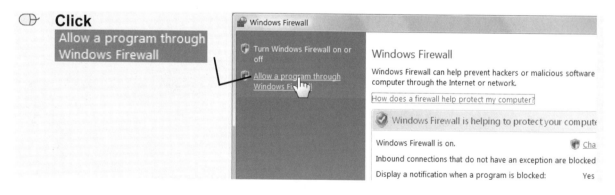

☞ **If necessary, give permission to continue**

For every program that is allowed, an exception will be added to this list:

You can enable the exception for a program by checking the box ☑ next to the program name: ────────

For now, you will not need to change these settings.

⊕ **Click** | Cancel |

Windows Firewall Settings

| General | Exceptions | Advanced |

Exceptions control how programs communicate through Windows Firewall. Add a program or port exception to allow communications through the firewall.

Windows Firewall is currently using settings for the domain network location.
What are the risks of unblocking a program?

To enable an exception, select its check box:

Program or port
☐ BITS Peercaching
☐ Connect to a Network Projector
☑ Core Networking
☑ Core Networking
☐ Distributed Transaction Coordinator
☑ File and Printer Sharing
☐ File and Printer Sharing
☐ iSCSI Service
☐ Media Center Extenders
☐ Netlogon Service
☐ Network Discovery
☐ Performance Logs and Alerts
☐ Remote Administration

| Add program... | Add port... | Properties | Delete |

☑ Notify me when Windows Firewall blocks a new program

| OK | Cancel | Apply |

☞ **Close the windows** ❀²

1.6 Setting Up the Windows Firewall in Windows XP

A *firewall* is a software or hardware component that regulates the ingoing and outgoing data traffic between your computer and the Internet and/or other networks. Depending on your firewall's settings, traffic is either blocked or allowed.

The word 'firewall' sounds a lot safer than it is. A firewall will not protect your computer from viruses. If the firewall allows your e-mail program to connect to the Internet, it is still possible to receive an e-mail message containing an attachment with a virus in it. The firewall does not check the contents of the data traffic.

⊕ **Click**

☞ **Click**  Security Center

☞ **Click** 🧱 Windows Firewall

You will see the *Windows Firewall* window:

Block all programs, except
the programs you have
selected: ———————

Block all programs, for
instance, in a public network:

Disable the firewall: ——————

☞ **Click the** Exceptions
tab —

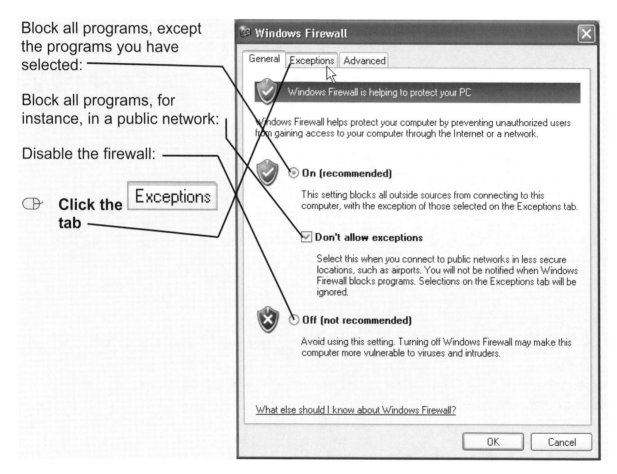

For every program that is allowed, an exception will be added to this list:

You can add a program to the exceptions list by checking the box ☑ next to the program:

For now, you will not need to change these settings.

In the bottom of the window:

☞ **Click** Cancel

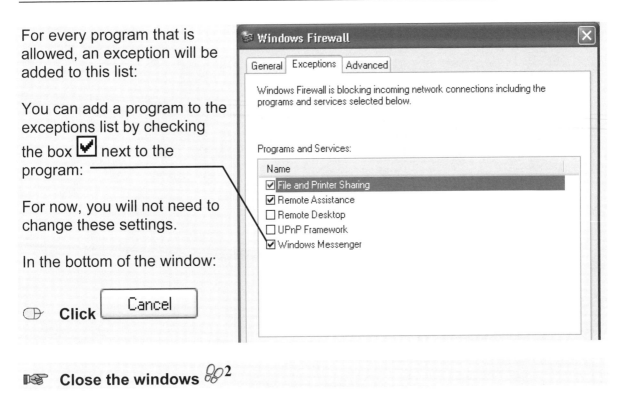

☞ **Close the windows** 👣²

1.7 Download and Install Microsoft Security Essentials

If you do not yet have an antivirus program installed, your computer will be in danger. If the license for your current antivirus program has expired and you cannot update the program any longer, your computer is also in danger. In that case, you will need to update the license as soon as possible, or buy a new antivirus program and install it.

Many antivirus programs offer free trial periods of thirty, sixty or even ninety days. In this way you can try the program and see if you like it before you purchase it. But there are also free antivirus programs that can be downloaded and installed from the Internet. In this section you can read how to download and install the free antivirus program *Microsoft Security Essentials*.

Please note:

If you already have an antivirus program installed and enabled on your computer, you can just read through this section. You may want to replace your old virus scanner with *Microsoft Security Essentials*. If you do this, it is important to follow the steps in the correct order. You can read more about this in *Appendix B Replacing the Antivirus Program*.

Please note:
Microsoft Security Essentials is suited for *Windows 7*, *Vista* and *XP*.

☉ Tip
Protection from viruses and spyware too
Microsoft Security Essentials detects and remove viruses, and it also removes spyware!

☞ **Open** *Internet Explorer* [1]

☞ **Open the www.microsoft.com/securityessentials website** [3]

You will see the button for downloading the program:

You can install the file right away:

You can install the file right away:

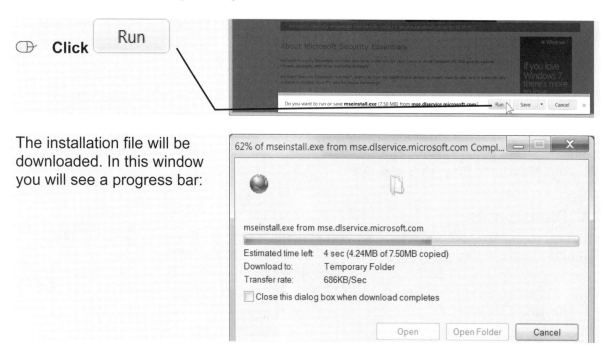

The installation file will be downloaded. In this window you will see a progress bar:

In *Windows XP* and *Windows Vista* you may also see a warning message:

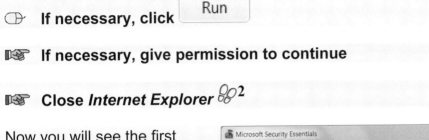 **If necessary, click** Run

☞ **If necessary, give permission to continue**

☞ **Close** *Internet Explorer* 👣²

Now you will see the first installation window of *Microsoft Security Essentials*:

 **Click** Next >

You will need to accept the user license terms:

Click I accept

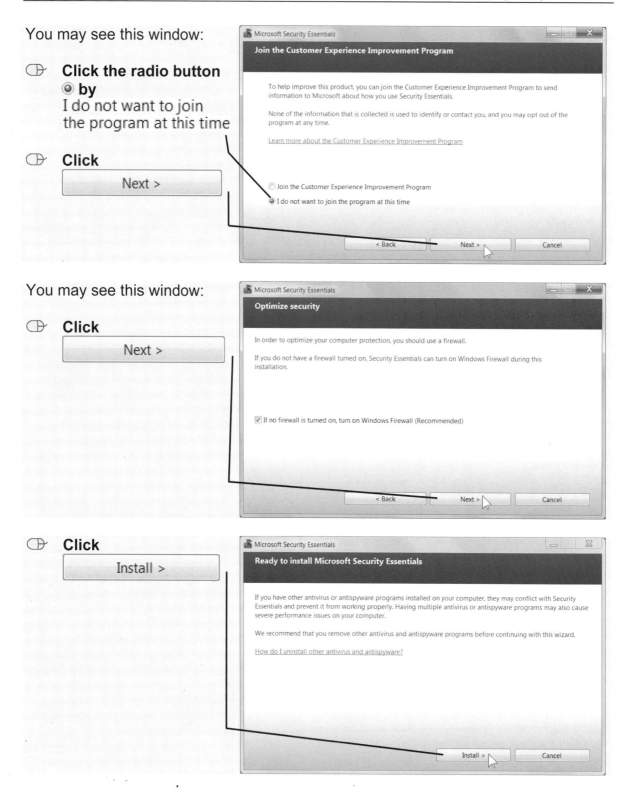

You may see this window:

☞ **Click the radio button**
   ◉ **by**
   I do not want to join
   the program at this time

☞ **Click**
   Next >

You may see this window:

☞ **Click**
   Next >

☞ **Click**
   Install >

Next, you will see a window indicating the progress of the download and install process. After the installation has been completed, you will see this window:

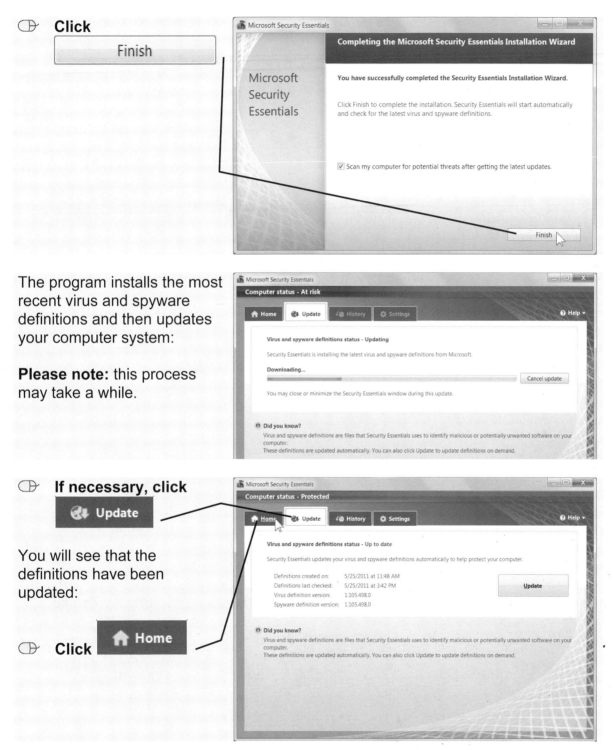

☞ **Click**

    Finish

The program installs the most recent virus and spyware definitions and then updates your computer system:

Please note: this process may take a while.

☞ **If necessary, click**

    Update

You will see that the definitions have been updated:

☞ **Click** Home

Now you will see the opening window of *Microsoft Security Essentials*:

At the top of the window you can see the current status:

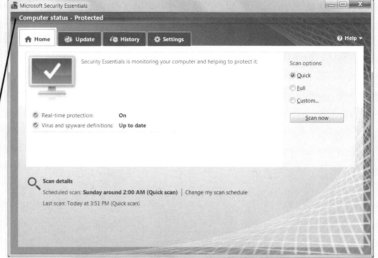

HELP! I do not see the Microsoft Security Essentials window

If you do not see the *Microsoft Security Essentials* window, you can open it in the following way:

Click

Click ▶ All Programs

Click Microsoft Security Essentials

To make sure that your computer has not been infected by a virus or other unwanted software, you can scan your computer:

You can select one of three types of scans:

- Quick: the program will only scan the locations where unwanted software has previously been detected;
- Full: the program will scan all the files and folders on your computer;
- Custom...: the program will only scan the folders you have selected.

1.8 Scanning Your Computer

To get an impression of how a scan works, you are going to let *Microsoft Security Essentials* execute a quick scan. This is how you do that:

☞ **Click the radio button**
   ◉ by *Quick*

☞ **Click**
   Scan now

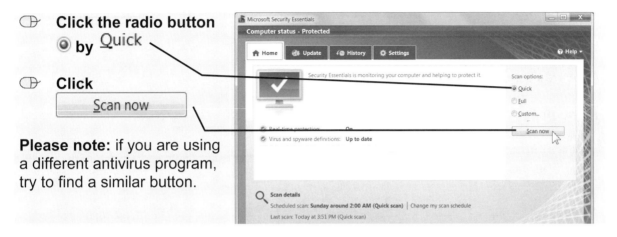

Please note: if you are using a different antivirus program, try to find a similar button.

Now your computer will be scanned for viruses. The duration of the scanning process will depend on the amount of files that need to be scanned.

While the program is scanning, you will see this window:

During the scanning process you will be able to use your computer in the usual way.

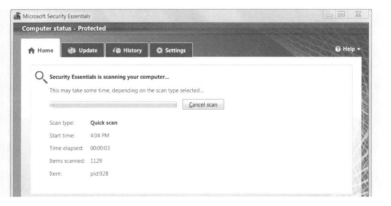

After the scan has finished, you will see a scan report.

In this example, no threats have been detected:

If no threats have been detected on your computer, you can just read through the next section.

If a harmful file has been detected, you will see this message:

You can view the details:

⊕ **Click** <u>Show details</u>

Please note: if you are using a different antivirus program, you will need to look for a similar button.

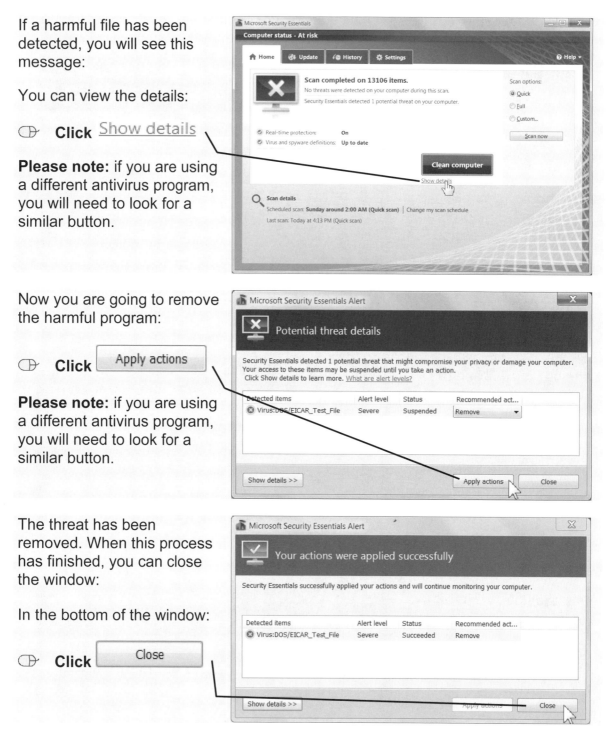

Now you are going to remove the harmful program:

⊕ **Click** | Apply actions |

Please note: if you are using a different antivirus program, you will need to look for a similar button.

The threat has been removed. When this process has finished, you can close the window:

In the bottom of the window:

⊕ **Click** | Close |

Tip

Windows Defender

Previously, you could use the free *Windows* program *Windows Defender* to detect and remove spyware. Now that *Microsoft Security Essentials* also detects and removes spyware, you no longer need *Windows Defender*.

That is why *Windows Defender* will automatically be disabled or uninstalled when you install *Microsoft Security Essentials*. Other anti-spyware programs that are activated simultaneously can hamper one another. This may cause a computer to crash, or slow down the computer.

If you use an antivirus program that does not detect spyware, you will also need to install a separate anti-spyware program. In this case you can use the *Windows Defender* program. In the PDF file called *Windows Defender Guide* you can read more about *Windows Defender*. You can download this file from our free downloads webpage: **www.visualsteps.com/info_downloads.php**

1.9 Changing the Settings for Microsoft Security Essentials

Instead of manually setting the start time for the scan, you can also schedule a time for the scan to start automatically.

Click
Change my scan schedule

Please note: if you are using a different antivirus program, look for a similar button.

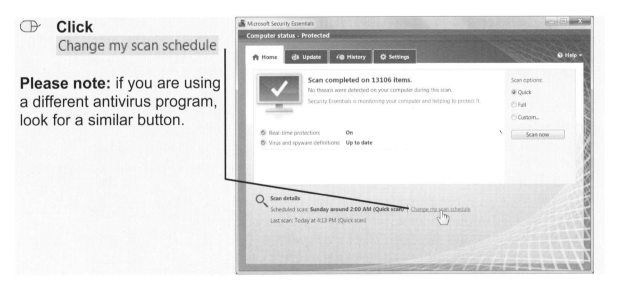

Now the *Settings* tab will be opened:

A weekly scan is scheduled
for Sunday 2.00 AM. If your
computer happens to not be
turned off at that time, the
scan will start the next time
you turn on your computer:

You can change these
settings, if you want.

Have you changed anything?

⊕ **Click** [🛡 Save changes]

Otherwise:

⊕ **Click** [Cancel]

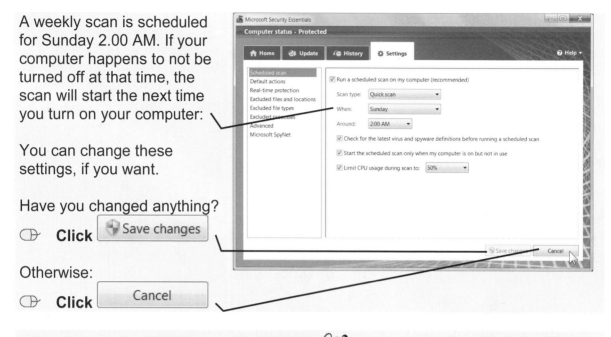

☞ **Close *Microsoft Security Essentials*** 👣²

💡 **Tip**

What to do with unwanted software
If you do not open unknown e-mail attachments, or use obscure programs, there is
very little chance that your computer will contract a virus. Nevertheless, your
antivirus program may find a suspect file now and then. In such a case, your
antivirus program will warn you and act immediately. The infected file will be
identified, the name of the virus will be displayed and the program will let you know
which type of action should be undertaken.

Most antivirus programs include three different types of actions:
• **Repair the file:** if a file on your computer has been infected, the program will try
  to repair the file by removing the virus. If it is an independent, isolated virus, such
  as a Trojan horse or a worm, it will be removed.
• **Place the file in quarantine:** the infected file or virus will not be removed, but
  moved to a separate folder where it cannot do any damage.
• **Remove the file:** the infected file or virus will be removed from your computer.
  This means that the contents of the file will be lost, unless you have made a
  backup copy. This is the usual course of action when there is no alternative
  solution for the problem.

1.10 Security Settings in Internet Explorer

In *Internet Explorer* you can create a safety level for Internet access. This way, you can determine how *Internet Explorer* should behave on different websites. In this book we use the screen shots from *Internet Explorer 9*. But the operations necessary for *Internet Explorer 8* will also be explained. However, this version is not compatible with *Windows XP*. Any possible differences with buttons, for example, in version 8 and 9 will be pointed out in the text.

Please note:

If you are still using *Internet Explorer 8*, you can switch to *Internet Explorer 9*. If you are using a *Windows XP* computer, you will not be able to install version 9. On the **www.visualsteps.com/info_downloads.php** webpage you will find a free booklet with information about *Internet Explorer 9*. In this booklet you can read how to download and install this latest version of *Internet Explorer*. If you are not sure which version of *Internet Explorer* you have, you can read how to check for it in section *1.20 Tips*.

Open *Internet Explorer* ⑧⑧¹

You are going to take a look at the security settings:

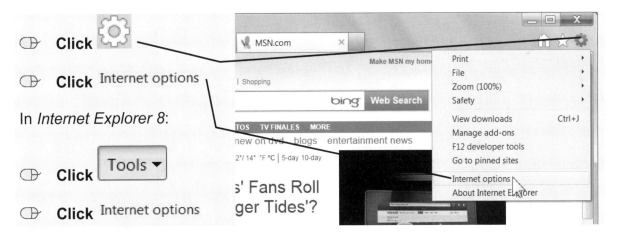

Click ⚙

Click Internet options

In *Internet Explorer 8*:

Click Tools ▼

Click Internet options

Now you will see the *Internet Options* window:

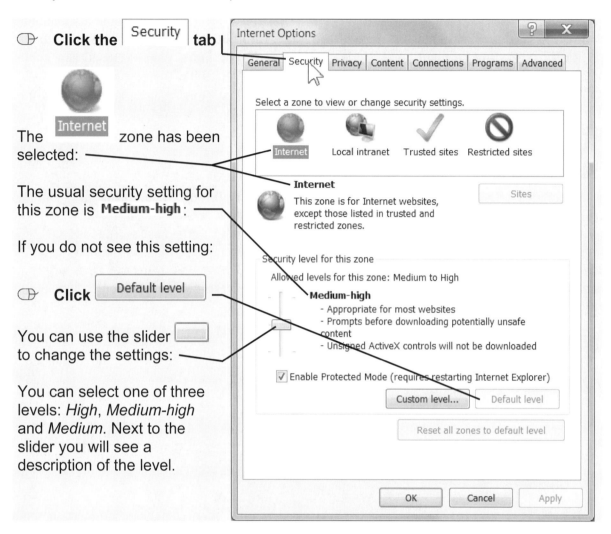

⊕ **Click the** Security **tab**

The Internet zone has been selected:

The usual security setting for this zone is **Medium-high**:

If you do not see this setting:

⊕ **Click** Default level

You can use the slider to change the settings:

You can select one of three levels: *High*, *Medium-high* and *Medium*. Next to the slider you will see a description of the level.

If necessary, you can select a different security setting for specific websites you do not trust, or do trust. Just take a look at the *Trusted sites*:

⊕ **Click** Trusted sites

You will see that the security level for this zone is set to **Medium** :

Again, you can use the slider to change the settings:

You can select one of five levels: *High*, *Medium-high*, *Medium*, *Medium-low* and *Low*.

The *Low* setting is only meant for websites which you completely trust.

To add a website to the *Trusted sites* zone:

⊕ **Click** | Sites |

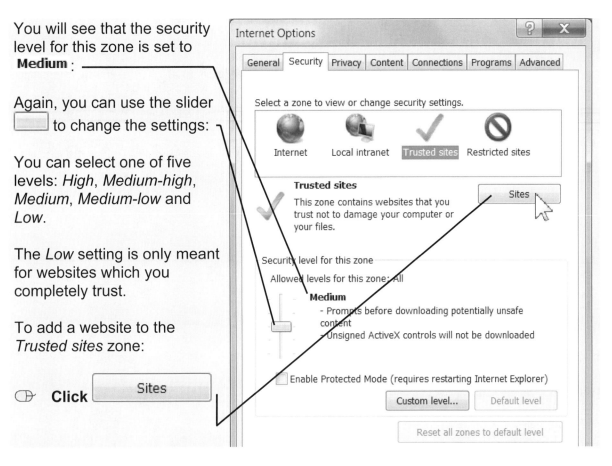

Internet Explorer assumes that you will want to add the website that is currently displayed in the window to your *Trusted sites*; this website will already be entered in the box *Add this website to the zone*. But you can also add a different website, for instance, your bank's website:

⊕ **Double-click the box by**
Add this website to the zone

⌨ **Type the address of your bank, for example,**
https://www.bankof
america.com

⊕ **Click** | Add |

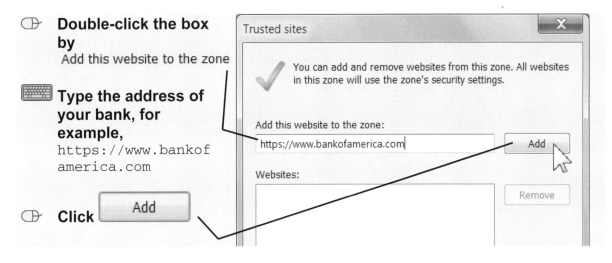

Please note:

The Require server verification (https:) for all sites in this zone setting means that the websites you add to the *Trusted sites* zone need to have the **https://** prefix. This prefix indicates that the connection is secure. The information that is exchanged between such a website and your computer is encrypted, and cannot be read by others.

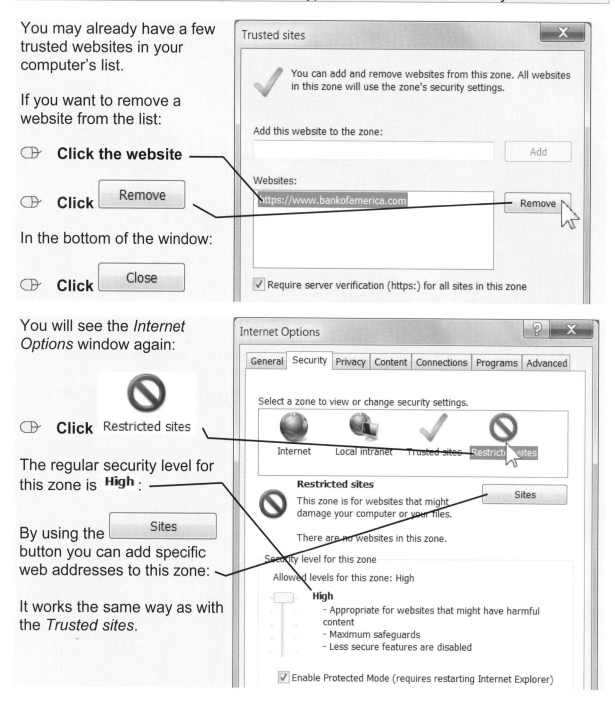

You may already have a few trusted websites in your computer's list.

If you want to remove a website from the list:

☞ **Click the website**

☞ **Click** Remove

In the bottom of the window:

☞ **Click** Close

You will see the *Internet Options* window again:

☞ **Click** Restricted sites

The regular security level for this zone is **High** :

By using the Sites button you can add specific web addresses to this zone:

It works the same way as with the *Trusted sites*.

1.11 Privacy Settings in Internet Explorer

In *Internet Explorer* you can also determine how your computer should deal with *cookies*. Cookies are small text files that are stored on your computer while you are surfing the Internet. These small files can contain information about the data you have entered while visiting certain web pages, for instance.

For example, if you book a trip with an online travel agency, their website will create a cookie that contains the dates and cities you have entered. This enables you to move forwards and backwards through the web pages, without having to re-enter the data on each page.

Note that these text files cannot be 'executed' or opened on your computer (these are not software programs) and their file size is quite small.

Please note:

Cookies are not dangerous. A website can only access the information that you have entered yourself. Once a cookie has been stored on your computer, it can only be accessed by the website that has created the cookie.

☞ **Click the** Privacy **tab**

The current privacy setting is **Medium** .
Under the caption you can read what this means:

If you do not see **Medium** :

☞ **Click** Default

Now you are going to view some additional settings for the cookies:

☞ **Click** Advanced

Internet Options

| General | Security | Privacy | Content | Connections | Programs | Advanced |

Settings

Select a setting for the Internet zone.

Medium

- Blocks third-party cookies that do not have a compact privacy policy
- Blocks third-party cookies that save information that can be used to contact you without your explicit consent
- Restricts first-party cookies that save information that can be used to contact you without your implicit consent

Sites   Import   Advanced   Default

Location

☐ Never allow websites to request your physical location   Clear Sites

Pop-up Blocker

☑ Turn on Pop-up Blocker   Settings

InPrivate

☑ Disable toolbars and extensions when InPrivate Browsing starts

You will see the *Advanced Privacy Settings* window:

In this example the cookies are handled automatically.

You can change this:

☞ **Check the box** ☑ **by**
    Override automatic cookie har

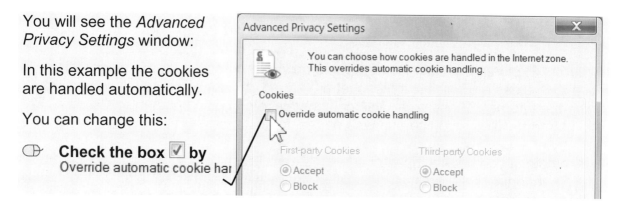

Now you can take a better look at the options. You can determine exactly what to do with *first-party cookies* and *third-party cookies*:

• **Accept**: cookies will be handled automatically;
• **Block**: not a single cookie will be accepted;
• **Prompt**: you will receive a message for each cookie and each time you will be asked whether you want to accept or block this cookie.

First-party cookies originate from websites you have visited; they can be persistent or temporary. A temporary cookie will be removed from *Internet Explorer* when you close the program. A persistent cookie will be stored on your computer and will remain there. The cookie will be retrieved and read the next time you visit the relevant website.

Indirect cookies originate from the advertisements on the websites you visit (such as *pop-ups* and *banners*). Websites can use these cookies to follow your Internet behavior and will use this information for marketing purposes.

In this example we are going to disable the automatic cookie handling.

But it is recommended to select the default setting.

☞ **Uncheck the box** ☑ **by**
    Override automatic cookie har

☞ **Click** OK

Advanced Privacy Settings

You can choose how cookies are handled in the Internet zone. This overrides automatic cookie handling.

Cookies

☐ Override automatic cookie handling

First-party Cookies
◉ Accept
○ Block
○ Prompt

Third-party Cookies
◉ Accept
○ Block
○ Prompt

☐ Always allow session cookies

OK   Cancel

🖐 **Please note:**

You may prefer to block all cookies. If you do that, however, there is always a chance that some websites will not function properly. Try different settings for a while. If you do not like the results, you can always revert back to the default setting.

💡 **Tip**

Always allow session cookies

Some websites use cookies while you are visiting the website, but will remove them afterwards. These are called *session cookies*. Session cookies are also temporary cookies. They are removed from your computer when you close *Internet Explorer*.

Session cookies are used for online banking, for instance. If you have set your browser to block all cookies, including session cookies, you will not be able to logon to the bank's website. The website will display a warning message.

This is why you always need to check the box ☑ next to
Always allow session cookies , even
if you want to block the other
cookies:

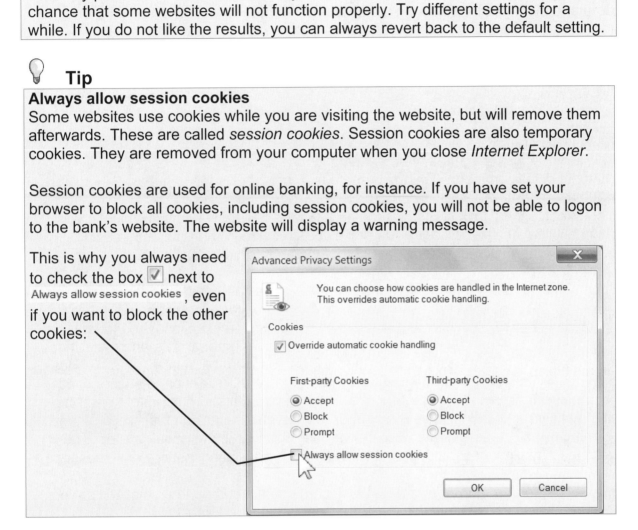

You can easily remove the cookies that are stored on your computer. In *section 2.1 Deleting the Browsing History* you can read more about this topic.

Have you changed any security or privacy settings? In the *Internet Options* window:

👉 **Click** OK

If you have not changed anything:

☞ **Close the *Internet Options* window** 🐾²

1.12 Phishing

More and more people are using the Internet these days, for online banking, shopping, booking a flight, selling used gear, studying, etcetera. Unfortunately, criminals have also found their way to the Internet. So-called *phishing* is one of the criminal activities that is on the rise.

What is phishing?
Online phishing is a method of persuading innocent computer users to hand over personal details or financial information. In fact, phishing is the same as 'fishing' for information.
A popular phishing trick starts by sending a fake e-mail message, which looks very much like the official messages you sometimes receive from trusted sources. For instance, your bank, your credit card company, an Internet shop or a website you once visited.
Such a message is sent to tens of thousands of e-mail addresses. In the e-mail message, the recipients are asked to check their bank data, for example. The mail will contain a hyperlink which leads to a website that is an exact copy of the genuine bank website. There you will be asked to confirm your personal data and enter them once again, such as your name and address, bank account numbers, or PIN codes. If you fall for this and enter the data, the information will be sent on to unscrupulous people who have set this trap. Next, they will use your data to purchase items, open new credit card accounts in your name, or abuse your identity in other ways. These phishing e-mail messages and websites are very similar to the genuine sites. The websites are expertly copied, and often the bank logo is used in the e-mail message.

Internet Explorer and *Windows (Live) Mail* both contain components that will protect you from phishing. This function does not exist in *Outlook Express*.

1.13 The SmartScreen Filter in Internet Explorer

In *Internet Explorer*, the *SmartScreen Filter* will help detect phishing websites. The *SmartScreen Filter* uses three methods to protect you from phishing activities:

- Comparison of the website address you visit with a list of websites that are listed as legal and 'good' websites by *Microsoft*.
- Analysis of the sites you have visited, in order to find out if these sites have the characteristics of a phishing website.
- On request of the user, *Microsoft* can check if a certain web address is listed in the list of recent phishing websites.

If the website you visit is listed in the list of reported phishing websites, *Internet Explorer* will display a warning page and a message on the address bar.
On this page you can continue or close the page.

If the website displays some characteristics of a phishing website, but is not listed, *Internet Explorer* will only display a message in the address bar, telling you this might be a phishing website is. This is how you open the *SmartScreen Filter* options:

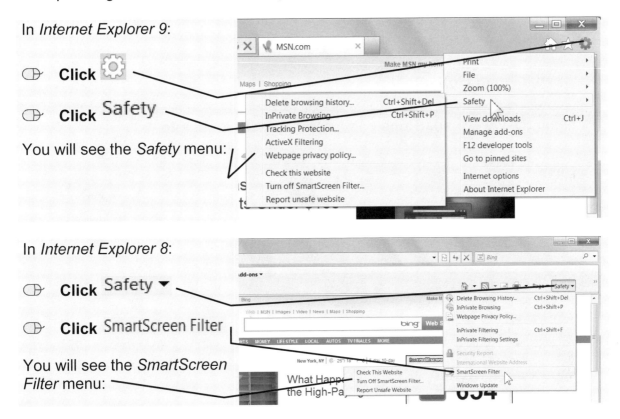

In *Internet Explorer 9*:

⬅️   **Click** ⚙️

⬅️   **Click** Safety

You will see the *Safety* menu:

In *Internet Explorer 8*:

⬅️   **Click** Safety ▼

⬅️   **Click** SmartScreen Filter

You will see the *SmartScreen Filter* menu:

In the menu you can select the following options:

- Check this website: if you do not trust the website you are visiting, you can use this option to check if the website is on the *Microsoft* list;
- Turn off SmartScreen Filter...: if you select this option, the websites you visit will no longer be checked. We strongly advise against this option;
- Report unsafe website: if a website is not stated as a suspect website or a phishing website, and you think the website is illegal, you can report this website to *Microsoft*.

☞   **Close** *Internet Explorer* ✂²

1.14 Pop-up Blocking

Pop-ups can be very annoying for Internet users. A pop-up is a small window that will be displayed on top of the website you are visiting. Pop-up windows have been developed by advertisers.

In *Internet Explorer*, you can use the option *Pop-up Blocking* to block pop-ups. If pop-up blocking is enabled and a pop-up is discovered, you will see an information bar.

☞ **Open *Internet Explorer*** ✌¹

☞ **Open the www.visualsteps.com/protect/practice website** ✌³

⊕ **Click** Pop-up

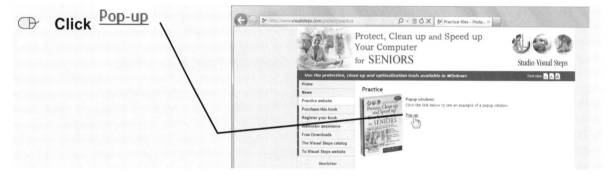

The website will try to display a pop-up window, and you will see an information bar:

In *Internet Explorer 9* you will see a notification window at the bottom of the page:

⊕ **Click**

> Options for this site ▼

In *Internet Explorer 8*:

⊕ **Click the information bar**

⊕ **Click** settings

⊕ **Click** More settings

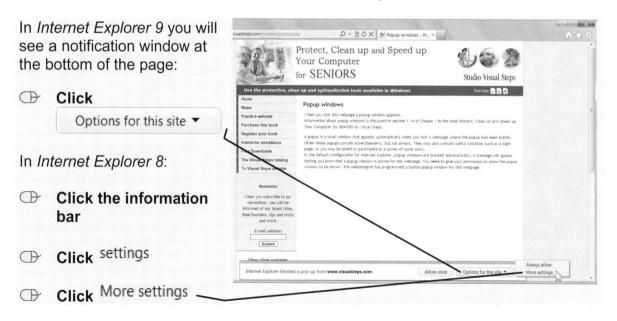

You can choose the blocking level: this ranges from blocking all pop-up windows to allowing all pop-ups.

In this case the filter level has been set to Medium:. This means that most of the pop-ups will automatically be blocked.

⊙ **By** Blocking level: **, click** Medium: Block most autom

You will see the other two filter levels:
High: Block all pop-ups (Ctrl+Alt to
and
Low: Allow pop-ups from secure s

⊙ **Click an empty spot in the window**

> **Pop-up Blocker Settings** [X]
>
> Exceptions
>
> Pop-ups are currently blocked. You can allow pop-ups from specific websites by adding the site to the list below.
>
> Address of website to allow:
>
> [   ] [Add]
>
> Allowed sites:
>
> [   ] [Remove]
>   [Remove all...]
>
> Notifications and blocking level:
> ☑ Play a sound when a pop-up is blocked.
> ☑ Show Notification bar when a pop-up is blocked.
>
> Blocking level:
> [Medium: Block most automatic pop-ups ▼]
> High: Block all pop-ups (Ctrl+Alt to overrid
> Medium: Block most automatic pop-ups
> Low: Allow pop-ups from secure sites

If you want to allow pop-ups from specific websites, you can enter the address here:

Afterwards, click the [Add] button to add the address to the list of allowed websites:

In this example you do not need to change the settings.

You can close the window. In the bottom of the window:

⊙ **Click** [Close]

> **Pop-up Blocker Settings** [X]
>
> Exceptions
>
> Pop-ups are currently blocked. You can allow pop-ups from specific websites by adding the site to the list below.
>
> Address of website to allow:
>
> [   ] [Add]
>
> Allowed sites:
>
> [   ] [Remove]
>   [Remove all...]
>
> Notifications and blocking level:
> ☑ Play a sound when a pop-up is blocked.
> ☑ Show Notification bar when a pop-up is blocked.
>
> Blocking level:

☞ **Close** *Internet Explorer* 👣²

1.15 Managing Add-ons in Internet Explorer

Add-ons
An *add-on* is a program that adds extra functions to a web browser, such as *Internet Explorer*. Examples of add-ons are extra toolbars, special mouse pointers and programs that block pop-ups. Add-ons are also known as *ActiveX controls*, *Plug-Ins*, *Browser Extensions* or *Browser Helper Objects*.

You can find and download many add-ons from the Internet. Usually you will need to give permission before they can be downloaded to your computer. But some add-ons are downloaded without you knowing it. This may happen when the add-on is component of a program you have installed. Some add-ons have been installed along with your *Windows* installation.

Normally, you can use add-ons without experiencing problems. But sometimes, an add-on may cause *Internet Explorer* to be closed unexpectedly. This may be the case when the add-on has been developed or built for a different version of *Internet Explorer*.

Here is how take a look at the add-ons you may have:

☞ **Open *Internet Explorer*** ✺¹

⊕ **Click** ⚙

⊕ **Click** Manage add-ons

In *Internet Explorer 8*:

⊕ **Click** Tools ▾

⊕ **Click** Manage add-ons

In the *Manage Add-ons*
window you can see which
add-ons have been loaded in
Internet Explorer.

Please note: the list in this
example will look different
from the list on your own
screen.

For each add-on, the name,
publisher and status will be
displayed.

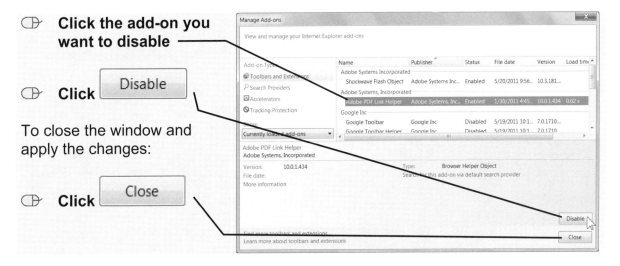

If you do not trust a certain add-on, or do not want to use it, you can disable it:

⊕ **Click the add-on you
want to disable**

⊕ **Click** [Disable]

To close the window and
apply the changes:

⊕ **Click** [Close]

To apply the changes you will usually need to close *Internet Explorer* first, and then
open it again:

☞ **Close** *Internet Explorer* ☙²

☞ **Open** *Internet Explorer* ☙¹

Now the add-on has been disabled.

If you decide to use the add-on once again, you can simply enable it:

☞ **Click** ⚙

☞ **Click** Manage add-ons

In *Internet Explorer 8*:

☞ **Click** Tools ▼

☞ **Click** Manage add-ons

☞ **Click the add-on you want to enable**

☞ **Click** Enable

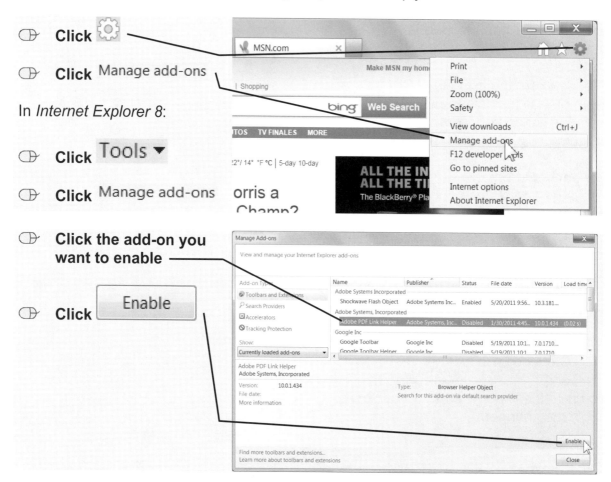

Now the add-on has been re-enabled. The change will be applied after you have closed and opened *Internet Explorer* again. Before closing the window, you can take a look at the add-ons on your computer which can be used by *Internet Explorer*:

☞ **By** Show:**, click** Currently loaded add-ons

☞ **Click** All add-ons

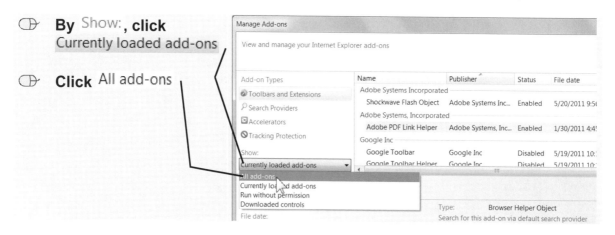

Now you will see the complete list of *Internet Explorer* add-ons.

Please note: the list on your screen will look different.

You do not need to change anything in this window:

⊕ **Click** [Close]

☞ **Close** *Internet Explorer* ℰℰ²

1.16 Filtering Unwanted E-mail in Windows 7

In *Windows Live Mail* the *Junk e-mail* filter will prevent phishing e-mails and other unwanted e-mails from entering your Inbox. These messages will be moved to the *Junk E-mail* folder.

⊕ **Click** 🔵 , All Programs , 📧 Windows Live Mail

If a message is suspected to be a phishing message or unwanted e-mail, it will be moved to the *Junk E-mail* folder and you will see a message:

⊕ **Click** [Close]

Here you can find the settings for the unwanted e-mail in *Windows Live Mail*:

⊕ **Click**

⊕ **Click** Options

⊕ **Click** 🛡 Safety options...

In this case, the protection level for junk e-mail is set to *Low:* :

This means that only the most obvious junk mail will be moved to the *Junk E-mail* folder.

You can select a higher protection level, but this may cause 'innocent' e-mails to end up in the *Junk E-mail* folder too:

The *Safe List Only:* options will only allow e-mail messages from addresses or domains on your *Safe Senders List* to be admitted to your *Inbox*:

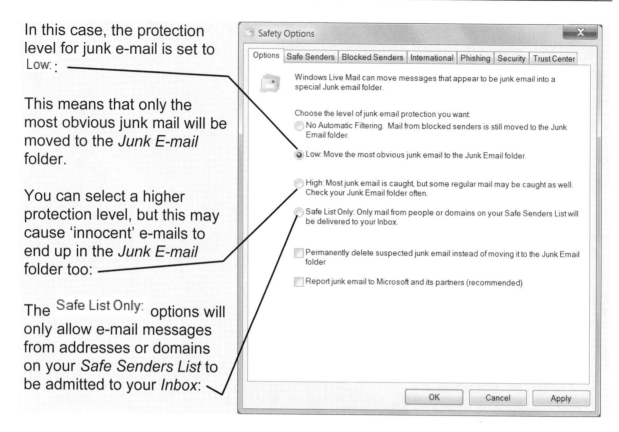

It is very easy to add e-mail addresses or domains to your *Safe Senders List*:

👆 **Click the** *Safe Senders* **tab**

👆 **Click** Add...

In the *Add address or domain* window you can enter this example:

⌨ **Type:**
visualsteps.com

👆 **Click** OK

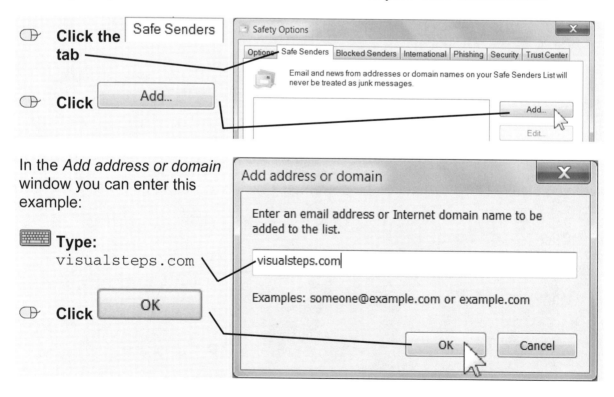

Now the *visualsteps.com* domain has been added to your *Safe Senders List*.

By using the ⎢ Blocked Senders ⎢ tab you can also add people or domains to the *Blocked Senders List*. E-mail messages sent by these people will automatically be moved to the *Junk E-mail* folder.

If you click the ⎢ Safe Senders ⎢ tab, you can move down to the bottom part of the window and specify which type of e-mail you want to trust. You can safely add addresses from the *Contacts* folder in *Windows Live Mail* and addresses of people with whom you have previously exchanged e-mails:

☞ **If necessary, check the box** ☑ **by**
  Also trust email from r

☞ **Check the box** ☑ **by**
  Automatically add peop

☞ **Click** ⎢ Apply ⎢

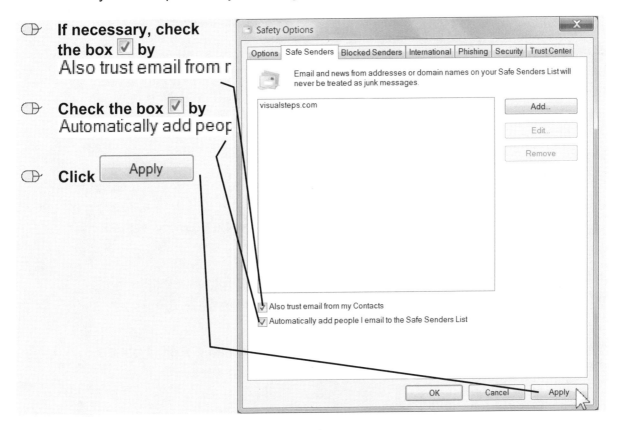

💡 Tip

No unwanted e-mail

The *Junk E-mail* filter cannot always tell the difference between junk e-mail and phishing e-mail. Once in awhile an innocent, harmless e-mail message will land in your *Junk E-mail* folder. That is why you should regularly check the *Junk E-mail* folder. If you find an e-mail that does not belong in that folder, you can use the

Not junk ▾ button in the *Windows Live Mail* window to move the selected message to

your *Inbox*. Otherwise use the Delete button to delete the message.

💡 Tip

Block international e-mails

If you click the International tab, you can specify tasks or domains and add them to the *Blocked Senders List*. If you receive messages in a different language, and no longer want to see these messages, you can use the Blocked Encoding List.. button to select that particular language.

You can use the Blocked Top-Level Domain List.. button to block all e-mail messages with a specific suffix. For example, an address ending with .mx or .ru.

If you click the Phishing tab, you can view the settings for possible phishing attempts.

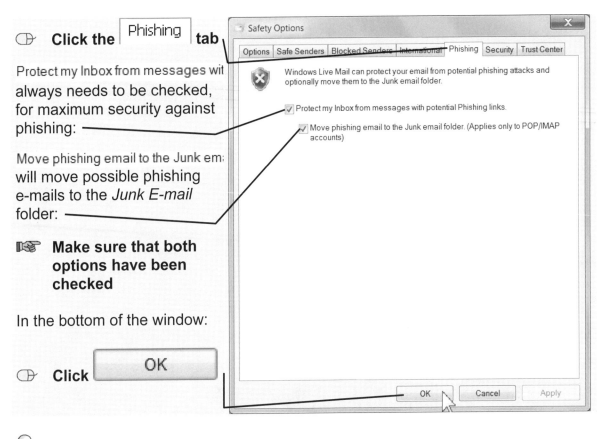

☞ **Click the** `Phishing` **tab**

Protect my Inbox from messages wit
always needs to be checked,
for maximum security against
phishing:

Move phishing email to the Junk em:
will move possible phishing
e-mails to the *Junk E-mail*
folder:

☞ **Make sure that both
options have been
checked**

In the bottom of the window:

☞ **Click** OK

💡 **Tip**

What else can I do to protect myself
Apart from the previously described options:

- Never enter your personal or financial information in an e-mail, chat message, or pop-up window. Your bank will never send an e-mail message asking you for your password or PIN code. Call the company or the organization, when you do not trust a certain message.
- Do not click hyperlinks in e-mails and chat messages sent by strangers, and do not click suspect links. Visit websites by typing the known address in the *Internet Explorer* address bar.
- Check if websites use a security code: a secure website will use the https:// prefix in the web address.
- Regularly check your bank and credit card statements.
- Report any suspect use of your personal information to the authorities.

On websites such as www.microsoft.com you can find additional information on phishing and well-known phishing activities.

☞ **Close *Windows Live Mail*** 🗇²

1.17 Filtering Unwanted E-mail in Windows Vista

Your Internet provider's spam filter will block much of the unwanted e-mail. But not everything is blocked. You may still find junk e-mail in your mailboxes. You can use message *rules* to move these messages to the *Junk E-mail* folder, but you can also simply block the sender. This is how you do that:

Click ⊙ , ▸ All Programs , 🗐 Windows Mail

➥ Please note:

Do you use *Windows Live Mail* on your *Windows Vista* computer? Then read *section 1.16 Filtering Unwanted E-mail in Windows 7*.

➥ Please note:

Blocking will not stop the messages from being sent, but will move them to the 🗐 Junk E-mail folder.

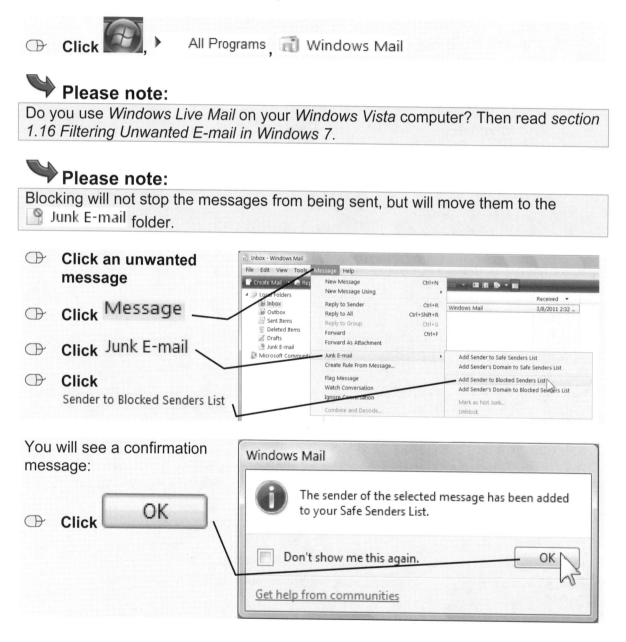

⊙ **Click an unwanted message**

⊙ **Click** Message

⊙ **Click** Junk E-mail

⊙ **Click** Sender to Blocked Senders List

You will see a confirmation message:

⊙ **Click** OK

➤ Please note:

It is possible that other messages from the same sender will also be moved to the  Junk E-mail folder.

➤ Please note:

In this same way you can also block domains, that is to say, the country code or suffix belonging to an Internet address. For instance, **.com** or .uk. But this will also prevent you from receiving e-mails sent by 'regular' addresses with that domain name. For example, if you block **.uk**, then all your mail from the United Kingdom will be perceived as junk e-mail.

In the *Junk E-mail Options* window you will find all the settings for blocking unwanted mail:

⊕ **Click** Tools

⊕ **Click**
    Junk E-mail Options...

You will see the options for letting *Windows Mail* filter your e-mail:

☞ **Select an option**

In this example we have selected Low:.

⊕ **Click the**
    Safe Senders **tab**

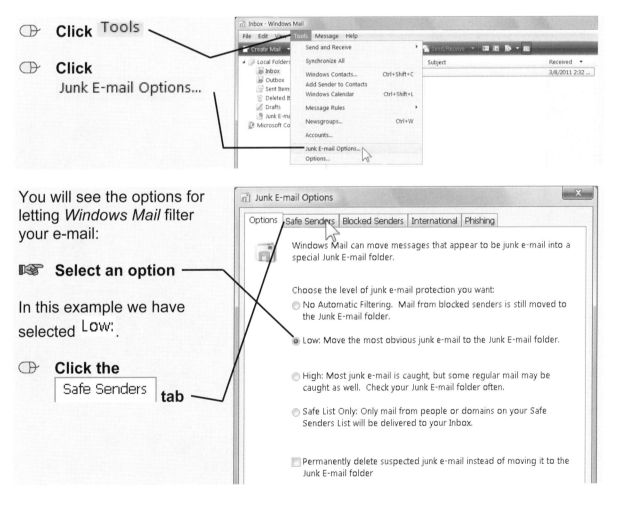

➥ Please note:

There is a greater chance of losing e-mail messages if you check the box ☑️ by Permanently delete suspected junk e-mail instead of moving it to the Junk E-mail folder .

Sometimes, regular e-mail is mistaken for spam, and if you let the program delete these messages as soon as they come in, you will never be able to check for this. If you let the program move the unwanted e-mail to the 🔋 Junk E-mail first, you will still be able to check if these messages are indeed junk.

Message from the senders listed here will always be accepted: —————

You will also want to receive the messages from your own contacts. So leave the Also trust e-mail from my Windows (option checked: ————

Now you are going to add new, safe, addresses:

🖙 **Click** Add...

🖮 **Type a safe address, for example,** info@visualsteps. com ————

🖙 **Click** OK

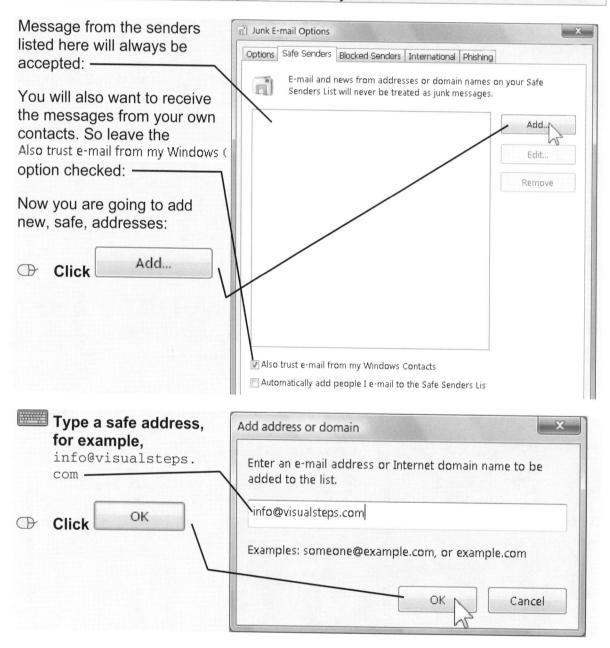

The address has been added.

To remove an address:

⊕ **Click the address**

⊕ **Click** Remove

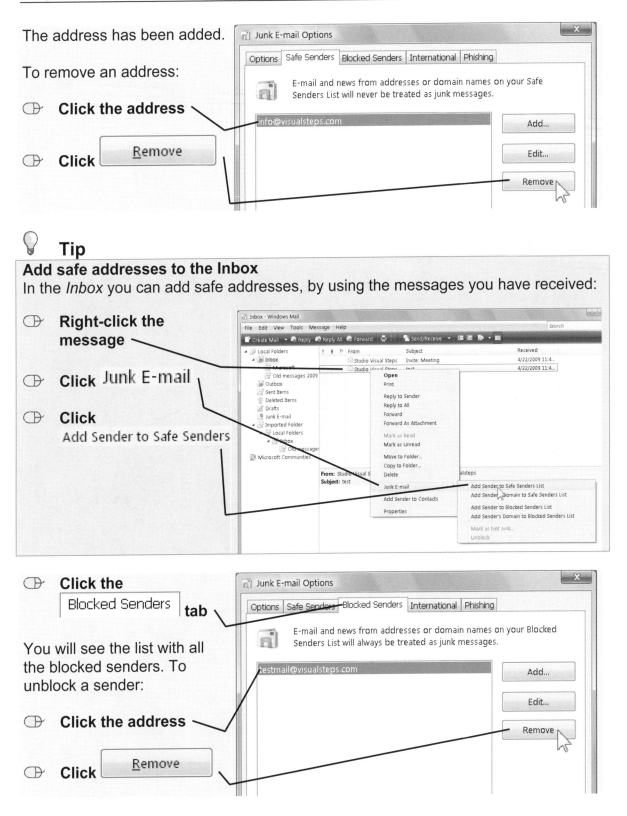

💡 **Tip**

Add safe addresses to the Inbox
In the *Inbox* you can add safe addresses, by using the messages you have received:

⊕ **Right-click the message**

⊕ **Click** Junk E-mail

⊕ **Click**
Add Sender to Safe Senders

⊕ **Click the**
Blocked Senders **tab**

You will see the list with all the blocked senders. To unblock a sender:

⊕ **Click the address**

⊕ **Click** Remove

Click the International tab

Here you can block the addresses with specific domain names.

Click

Blocked Top-Level Domain List.

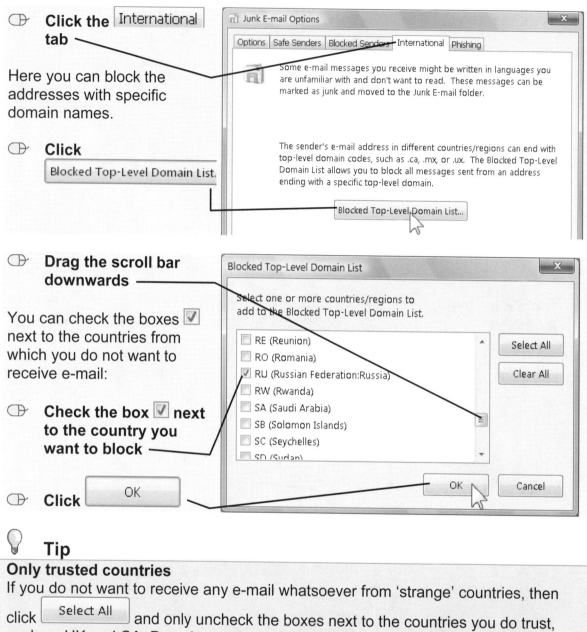

Drag the scroll bar downwards

You can check the boxes ☑ next to the countries from which you do not want to receive e-mail:

Check the box ☑ next to the country you want to block

Click OK

💡 **Tip**

Only trusted countries
If you do not want to receive any e-mail whatsoever from 'strange' countries, then click Select All and only uncheck the boxes next to the countries you do trust, such as UK and CA. Domains such as .COM, .ORG and .EDU will not be blocked.

A lot of spam originating from specific countries does not use the domain name of this country, but will use a domain name such as .com, for example. It is not recommended to block .com senders, because many trusted companies use a .com address. People who send spam will change the address regularly, so there is simply no point in blocking the sender. But you can block the e-mail from non-western languages, for instance Cyrillic languages such as Russian.

Here is how you do that:

In the bottom of the window:

☞ **Click**

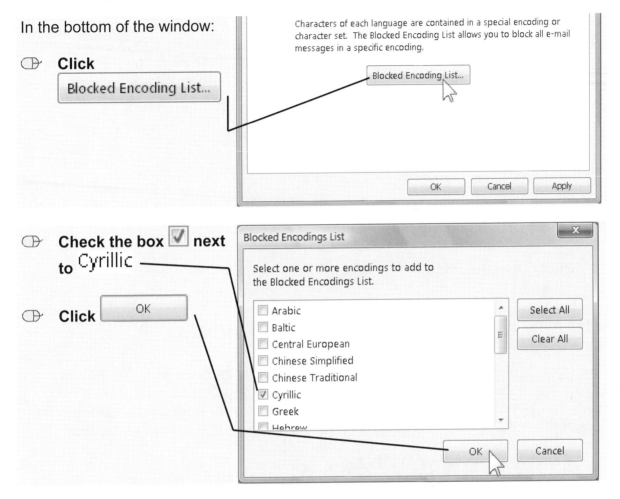

From now on, all e-mails containing Cyrillic script will be blocked. Now you can take a look at the *Phishing* settings:

Phishing is a fraudulent method for sending e-mails that present themselves as legitimate messages from a bank, or another trusted company. In the message you will be asked to click a link that will lead you to the forged website of the bank in question. There you will be asked to enter confidential information, such as passwords, pin numbers or other codes.

This data is used by criminals, to purchase items at your expense, or to transfer money from your account. It is recommended that you keep this protection activated. Keep in mind that the phishing protection is not 100% guaranteed. You need to be on the lookout for these fake messages yourself.

To save the settings:

☞ **Click** [OK]

To cancel the changed settings:

☞ **Click** [Cancel]

☞ **Close** *Windows Mail* 👣²

1.18 Filtering Unwanted E-mail in Windows XP

Your Internet provider's spam filter will block a lot of unwanted e-mail. But not all e-mails are blocked. This means you may find some unwanted e-mail in your mailboxes, once in a while. You can use message *rules* to move these e-mails to the *Deleted Items* folder, but you can also block the sender. This is how you do that:

☞ **Click** [start] , [All Programs ▶] , 🗐 Outlook Express

🢒 **Please note:**

Blocking will not stop the messages from being sent, but will move them to the 🗑 Deleted Items folder.

☞ **Click** 🗐 **Inbox**

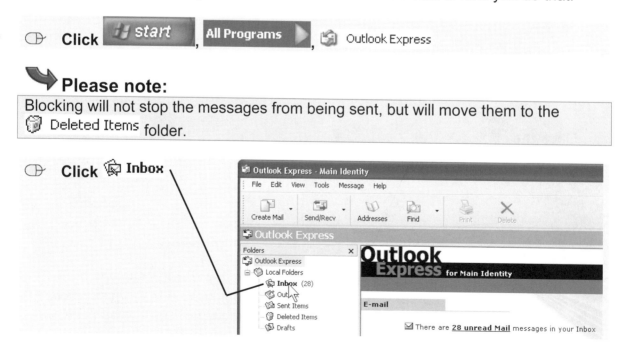

☞ **Click an unwanted message**

☞ **Click** Message

☞ **Click** Block Sender...

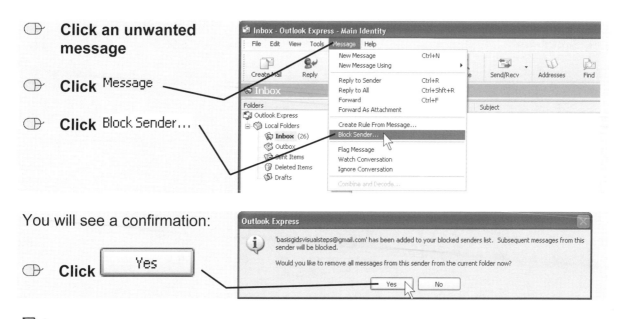

You will see a confirmation:

☞ **Click** [Yes]

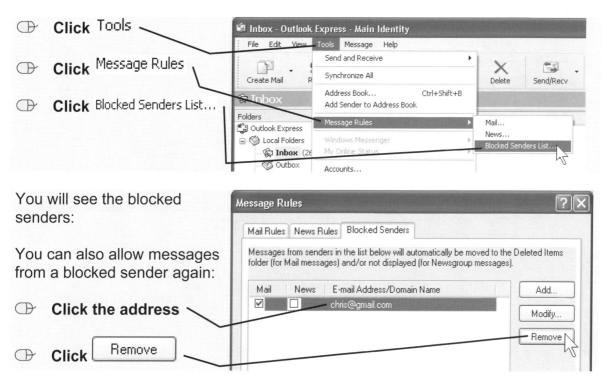

Please note:

By confirming this message you will move any other messages from this same sender to the 🗑 Deleted Items folder.

You can also manually block senders, or remove senders from the blocked senders list:

☞ **Click** Tools

☞ **Click** Message Rules

☞ **Click** Blocked Senders List...

You will see the blocked senders:

You can also allow messages from a blocked sender again:

☞ **Click the address**

☞ **Click** [Remove]

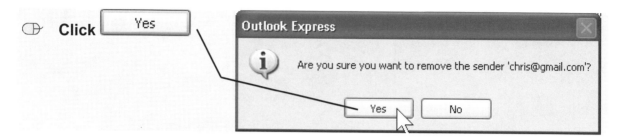

⊕ **Click** [Yes]

You can also manually add a sender:

⊕ **Click** [Add...]

Now you will see a window in which you can add a sender. This can be an e-mail address or a domain name:

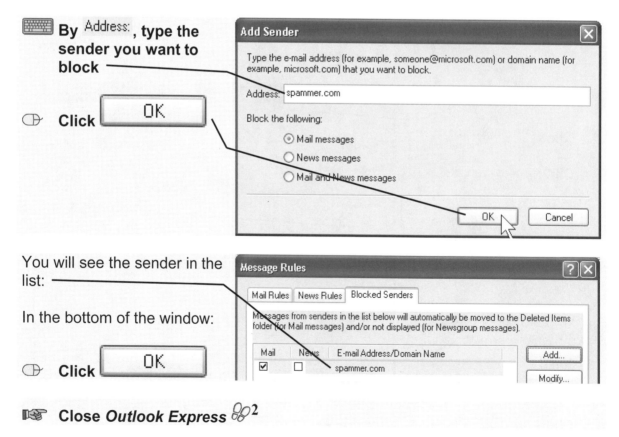

⌨ **By** Address: **, type the sender you want to block**

⊕ **Click** [OK]

You will see the sender in the list:

In the bottom of the window:

⊕ **Click** [OK]

☞ **Close** *Outlook Express* 𝒫2

1.19 Background Information

Dictionary

Action Center	System that checks your computer's security settings and the *Windows updates* in *Windows 7*.
Add-on	A program that adds functions to an Internet browser, such as *Internet Explorer.*
Cookie	A small text file that a website stores on your computer containing information about you and your preferences.
Custom scan	The option in an antivirus or antispyware program which allows you to scan only the folders you have selected.
Direct cookies	Direct cookies originate from the website you are currently visiting. These cookies can be persistent or temporary. Websites can use these cookies to store information which they will use the next time you visit this website.
Filter Junk E-mail	In *Windows Live Mail* and *Windows Mail*, the *Junk E-mail* filter will move phishing e-mails and other unwanted messages to the *Junk E-mail* folder.
Firewall	A firewall is software or hardware that protects your computer by checking information coming from the Internet or a network, and then either blocks it or allows it to pass through to your computer. This depends on your firewall settings.
Full scan	Option in an antivirus or antispyware program wherein all files and folders on your computer will be scanned.
Https://	If you see this prefix preceding a web address, the Internet connection is secure (encrypted data traffic).
Indirect cookies	Indirect cookies originate from advertisements (such as pop-up advertisements and banners) on the website you are currently viewing.
Junk e-mail	Unwanted, commercial e-mail, also known as *spam*.
Microsoft Security Essentials	Total solution for your Internet security. The program protects your computer from viruses, but also offers firewall and antispyware protection.

- Continue on the next page -

Phishing	Phishing is the practice of sending a fraudulent e-mail message to induce a computer user to reveal personal or financial information. A common online phishing scam starts with an e-mail message that looks like an official notice from a trusted source, such as a bank, credit card company, or reputable online merchant. In the e-mail message, recipients are directed to a fraudulent website where they are asked to provide personal information, such as an account number or password.
Pop-up	A pop-up is a small browser window that appears on top of the website you're viewing. Pop-up windows often open as soon as you visit a website and are frequently used by advertisers.
Pop-up blocking	Pop-up blocking is an option in *Internet Explorer* that lets you restrict or block pop-ups from being displayed.
Quick scan	Option in an antivirus or antispyware program. By running this type of scan you only scan the locations where unwanted software has previously been detected.
Security Center	System that checks your computer's security settings as well as the *Windows updates* in *Windows Vista* and *Windows XP*.
SmartScreen Filter	In *Internet Explorer*, the *SmartScreen Filter* will help protect you from phishing websites. If the website is listed in the list of reported phishing websites, the address bar will display a message.
Spam	Unwanted, commercial e-mail.
Spyware	Software that can display advertisements (such as pop-up advertisements), or collect personal information, or even change your computer's settings without asking for your permission.
Temporary cookies	Temporary cookies or session cookies will be removed from your computer when you close *Internet Explorer*. Websites use these cookies to store temporary information. For example, the items added to a shopping cart when visiting an online store.
Trojan horse	A Trojan horse is a malicious software program that hides inside other programs. It enters a computer hidden inside a legitimate program, such as a screen saver. It does not appear to be harmful, but will cause damage when it is executed.
Unwanted software	Programs that are designed to harm your computer.

- Continue on the next page -

Virus	A virus is a program that replicates itself and tries to spread from one computer to another. It can cause damage (by deleting or damaging data) or annoy the user (by displaying messages or altering the information on the screen).
Windows Defender	Antispyware program that is included in *Windows*, or can be downloaded for use in *Windows*. This program has become redundant since the release of *Microsoft Security Essentials*.
Worm	A program that reproduces itself, just like a virus. Criminals can use worms to take over your computer.

Source: Windows Help and Support

Surf safely

In this chapter you have learned about various security settings in *Windows*. But do not forget that your own behavior plays an important part in your computer's security.

Here is a list of things to keep in mind:

- Make sure your antivirus program is up to date.
- Make sure you use a good firewall.
- Make sure that *Windows* is up to date.
- Use *Microsoft Security Essentials*, *Windows Defender* or a different antispyware program to remove spyware from your computer.
- Regularly scan your computer with the antivirus and antispyware programs.
- If something strange happens while you are surfing the Internet, immediately disconnect from the Internet.
- If you do not use your Internet connection, then disconnect. This reduces the chance of others breaking in to your computer.
- Protect your computer from pop-ups, junk e-mail and phishing, by using the settings we have discussed in this chapter.
- Only download files and programs from trusted websites.

- Continue on the next page -

- Do not enter a lot of information when visiting websites. Never enter personal/financial information (credit card data, bank account information, PIN codes or passwords), unless you are 100% positive that the website can be trusted.
- Avoid entering your e-mail address by every website that requests it. Some websites try to collect e-mail addresses in order to send spam to these addresses at a later stage. Use a free e-mail account, such as *Hotmail*, *Windows Live Mail*, or *Gmail*, when you are asked to enter an e-mail address on the Internet. Or use the spam-mail address given to you by your provider.
- Pay attention to the web address and the security settings of the websites when you want to purchase items online, or access your online bank account. The address (URL) should contain the exact, correct name and start with https://.

Shopping and paying on the Internet

Just like in the real world, the customer and the supplier want to be sure everything is above board when buying and selling on the Internet. The customer wants the goods to be delivered in good order, and the supplier wants to be paid. The supplier will ask the customer to provide some information. He will need to know where to send the goods and will want to know who is responsible if the payment fails to come through.

How can I pay online?

- **Cash on delivery** – You will pay the bill directly to the delivery person, when the goods are delivered to your home. Make sure to check the contents of the package before you sign anything, or pay the bill.
- **By invoice** – You place an order and then the Internet store sends you the bill. After you have paid, the goods will be sent to you. Some shops will send the invoice and ship the goods all at the same time.
- **By standing order** – You authorize the company to withdraw the amount from your bank account. This has the advantage that you can usually revoke the payment within fourteen days, if you think the order has not been carried out according to your wishes.
- **PayPal** – This is a popular Internet payment service, used by auction websites and other online retailers. You can use PayPal to authorize payment via the e-mail address of the recipient, combined with the use of a credit card, or by using money that has been previously transferred to your PayPal account. You can also transfer money from a PayPal account to a bank account. On the www.paypal.com website you can find additional information about this payment method.

Safe e-mail behavior

A regular e-mail message, containing only text should not pose much of a threat. But an attachment to an e-mail message can be dangerous. Fortunately, several types of potentially dangerous attachments will be blocked directly by the security settings in *Windows Live Mail* (*Windows 7*), *Windows Mail (Windows Vista)* and *Outlook Express* (*Windows XP*). But it is extremely important that you take a close look at your messages before opening them.

Make sure to check these things:

- Always use an antivirus program that is up to date.
- Never open messages from unknown senders. Delete them immediately.
- Does the subject of a message look familiar to you? Sometimes, viruses use old messages and send these to random addresses in the *Contacts* folder on the infected computer. If you think the message is old or not intended for you, then delete it immediately. You can also try to call the sender first.
- Does the message contain an attachment with a weird name or a strange file type? Do not be curious, just delete it immediately.
- First, view the contents of a message in the preview window, before double-clicking to open it.
- Does the message concern spectacular offers, prizes or miracle cures? Never answer these messages and never click any possible links in the message. By reacting to the message, you will let the sender know that your e-mail address is in use. This will only increase the amount of spam.
- The *SmartScreen Filter* is not able to detect each and every phishing message. Never answer e-mails sent to you by banks, credit card companies or Internet shops, where they ask you to enter personal information. These e-mail messages may look very authentic, but they will always be fake messages.
- Be careful with your e-mail address. Do not give it to just anybody. Do not enter it on random websites. Before you know it, you will receive all sorts of spam and unwanted messages. There is a brisk trade in e-mail addresses going on.
- Consider acquiring an extra e-mail address. Your first address is for friends, family and your work-related contacts. You can use the second address for use on various websites. If you receive too many messages with this second address, you can always get a third address.
- Keep in mind that deleted messages will be stored in the *Junk E-mail* folder, and that you need to empty this folder from time to time.

Hoaxes and chain letters

Hoaxes and *chain letters* are e-mail messages that are written for one sole purpose. That is, trying to get you to send these messaged to everyone you know. Usually, the contents of these messages are completely false.

Hoaxes are e-mails that contain a fake virus alert. Often, the message will give a detailed description of how to search your hard disk for a specific virus file and how to delete this virus. In many cases, this file will be a *Windows* system file. If you were to follow the instructions, it is possible that *Windows* will no longer function properly. Never follow these instructions, and do not forward these messages to others.

Here is an example of such a hoax-mail:

"Dear Everybody!
To all friends and acquaintances and everybody in my address book. Currently, a new virus has been discovered. Unfortunately, my computer has been infected too. This virus is not detected by Norton and McAfee. Neither by the e-mail virus scan of my provider. The virus will lay dormant for about 14 days before damaging your computer; it will automatically be forwarded to the contacts in your address book, whether you send an e-mail or not.
AS SOON AS YOU DETECT THE VIRUS YOU WILL NEED TO WARN ALL THE CONTACTS IN YOUR ADDRESS BOOK, EVEN IF YOU HAVE NOT SENT ANY E-MAILS LATELY. YOUR CONTACTS CAN THEN WARN THEIR OWN CONTACTS AND FRIENDS. This is what you need to do:.." etcetera.

Other types of hoaxes will contain stories about people who are ill or need help. By sending these messages to others, the senders try to raise money. These messages are almost always unreliable and are only intended to make money.

Chain letters use the same set-up as hoaxes. Usually, these messages promise you money or happiness, if you forward them. Chain letters are often used as a way of collecting e-mail addresses to be sold later to commercial companies.

Usually, you will receive a hoax or a chain letter from a known sender. This enhances the credibility of the story and may even get you to believe it. Always check the information in the e-mail yourself. A good reference site for this information is http://urbanlegends.about.com or www.hoax-slayer.com.

Always warn the person who sent the hoax e-mail to you that it is about a fake virus, and draw attention to the websites mentioned above.

1.20 Tips

💡 Tip

Blocking Flash pop-ups

Previously, in this chapter you have read how to change the settings in *Internet Explorer* to block pop-ups. With these settings, most pop-ups will be blocked. But these settings only apply to pop-ups that have been created with the JavaScript programming language. There also exist pop-ups that have been created with Flash. These pop-ups will not be blocked by the method learned earlier, but there is another method to use for blocking Flash pop-ups. Here is how to apply the setting:

In *Internet Explorer 9*:

☞ **Click** ⚙

☞ **Click** Manage add-ons

In *Internet Explorer 8*:

☞ **Click** Tools ▼

☞ **Click** Manage add-ons

In *Windows 7*:

☞ **By** Show: **, select the** Currently loaded add-ons **option** ⎯

☞ **Click** Shockwave Flash Object

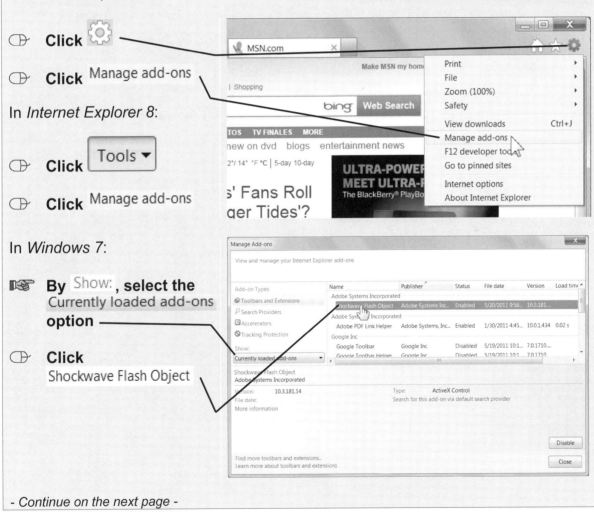

- Continue on the next page -

In the bottom right of the window:

Type: ActiveX Control
Search for this add-on via default search provider

🖱 **Click** | Disable |

Disable

🖱 **Click** | Close |

ions...
extensions

Close

☞ **Close** *Internet Explorer* 🦶²

☞ **Open** *Internet Explorer* 🦶¹

Now the add-on has been disabled. Flash pop-ups will no longer be displayed. At the same time, other Flash applications will be blocked too, which can be a problem. In *Internet Explorer*, many videos or online browser games also use Flash, and now you will not be able to view them. If you want to use these applications, you will need to temporarily re-activate the Shockwave Flash Object add-on. You can do that by following the instructions in *section 1.15 Managing Add-ons in Internet Explorer*.

💡 **Tip**

Antivirus programs
If you do not want to use *Microsoft Security Essentials*, there are other good antivirus programs that you can buy. The best-known security programs are *Norton* and *McAfee.* But less well-known programs such as *Norman* or *Panda* will also do a good job. These programs offer a free trial period of fifteen, thirty or sixty days.

For additional information, visit these websites:
- *McAfee*: www.mcafee.com
- *Norton*: www.symantec.com
- *Norman*: www.norman.com
- *Panda*: www.pandasecurity.com

🔆 Tip

How to recognize a secure website

Whenever you buy something on the Internet, you will always need to check whether the website is secure, before entering your bank account information.

The main difference between a secure website and an unprotected website is that the information on a secure website is sent by means of encoding technology. The user enters his or her data, such as a credit card number. This information is encoded (encrypted) by using special software programs and then handed over to the supplier, who can decode the information. Only authorized parties can decode the information. In this way, companies try to prevent hackers from stealing information that is sent over the Internet.

The easiest and fastest way of recognizing a secure website, is by looking at the web address in the *Internet Explorer* address bar. If the web address starts with https:// instead of http://, you can be sure that this is a secure website. The extra 's' stands for 'secure'.

Here is an example:

Another sign of a secure site is the small 🔒 symbol that is displayed in the address bar, as soon as you open the website. If you do not see this symbol, there is a good chance of the website not being secure.

Please note: many websites contain a secure section as well as an unprotected section. For instance, if you are reading information about a book at www.amazon.com or clothing at www.llbean.com, these pages will not be secure. But once you decide to actually purchase an item, the checkout procedure begins and you will be lead to the secure section of the website.

Only enter your personal details and credit card information if you are sure that you are visiting a website that guarantees a secure method of communication.

Tip

Check your version of Internet Explorer

To be able to perform all the actions explained in this book, you will need to use *Internet Explorer 8* or *Internet Explorer 9*.

On our free downloads webpage **www.visualsteps.nl/info_downloads.php**, you will find a booklet that explains how to switch to *Internet Explorer 9*. In this booklet we explain how to download and install this latest version of *Internet Explorer*.

If you think this job is too difficult, ask your computer supplier for help, or ask a more experienced person that you know to help you.

Are you not sure of which version you are using? This is how to check which version you have:

☞ **Open *Internet Explorer* 🕮¹**

If the top of the window looks like this, you are using *Internet Explorer 9*:

If the top of the window looks like this, you are using *Internet Explorer 8*:

In that case you can install *Internet Explorer* version 9.

Please note: *Internet Explorer 9* is not compatible with *Windows XP*.

2. Clean Up

When you surf the Internet with *Internet Explorer*, information about the websites you visit is stored on your computer. This can enhance your browsing speed. But there are times where it is useful to know how to remove this information. For example, when you have been surfing on a public computer.

After using your computer for a while, you may find that you have accumulated a lot of programs that you hardly ever use. It is a good idea to remove these programs, so they will not clutter up your computer.

When you work with a multitude of programs and files, the information will be scattered about and stored in different locations on your computer's hard drive. This will cause your computer to become increasingly slower. You can alleviate this problem by regularly cleaning up your computer and *defragmenting* your hard drive. You can use the *Analyze Disk* option in *Windows* to check if your hard drive is functioning properly.

The *System Restore* program keeps track of changes in the operating system, and in some of the application files. You can use so-called *restore points* to repair the system by restoring it to a previous version.

In this chapter you will learn how to:

- delete the browser history from *Internet Explorer*;
- remove a program;
- clean up your computer;
- use *Analyze Disk*;
- defragment your hard drive;
- create restore points;
- restore the system from a restore point.

Please note:

To execute all the operations that are described in this chapter, you will need to use the administrator's account (be logged in as administrator). If you cannot use this account, you will not be able to change several settings. When this happens, *Windows* will display a warning message. In such a case you can just read through the relevant section.

➥ **Please note:**

The screen shots in this chapter have been made in *Internet Explorer 9*. If any of the operations are different in *Internet Explorer 8*, they will also be explained. Are you using an older version of *Internet Explorer*? Would you like to upgrade to version 9? See *section 1.20 Tips* for more information about *Internet Explorer 9*.

2.1 Deleting the Browsing History

When you surf the Internet, *Internet Explorer* automatically stores information about the websites you visit. This information may include data you have entered on a website, such as your name and address. The browsing history can contain any of the following elements:

- **Temporary Internet files**: the first time you access a webpage, it will be stored in the *Temporary Internet Files* folder. This will speed up the loading of the page the next time you visit it. *Internet Explorer* uses your internet connection to check for any changes to the website and if none are found loads the webpage from the *Temporary Internet Files* folder of your computer.
- **Cookies**: small text files, stored on your computer by various websites; these files contain information about you and your preferences.
- **History**: a list of all the websites you have visited.
- **Form data**: information that you have entered in web forms, or in the address bar (such as your name, address, and web addresses).
- **Passwords**: each time you enter a password on a website, *Internet Explorer* will ask you if you want to store this password. These stored passwords can also be deleted.

Normally, it is quite useful to have this information stored on your computer, because it will speed up the surfing process and save time by reducing the need of having to re-enter certain types of information, such as login codes. You can delete this information from your computer at any time and without much hassle. It is good idea to adopt this practice after using a public computer so that no trace of your personal information is left behind.
This is how you delete the browsing history:

☞ **Open** *Internet Explorer* ✂¹

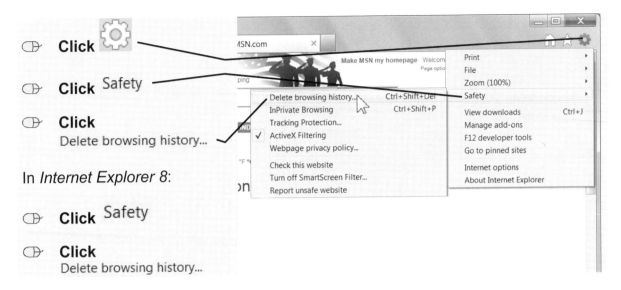

⊕ **Click** ⚙

⊕ **Click** Safety

⊕ **Click**
Delete browsing history...

In *Internet Explorer 8*:

⊕ **Click** Safety

⊕ **Click**
Delete browsing history...

In the following window you can select which part of the browsing history you want to delete.

If you want to delete the history of the websites you have visited:

⊕ **Uncheck the boxes** ☑ **next to**
Temporary Internet files and Cookies

You can leave the box ☑ next to **History** checked:

In the bottom of the window:

⊕ **Click** Delete

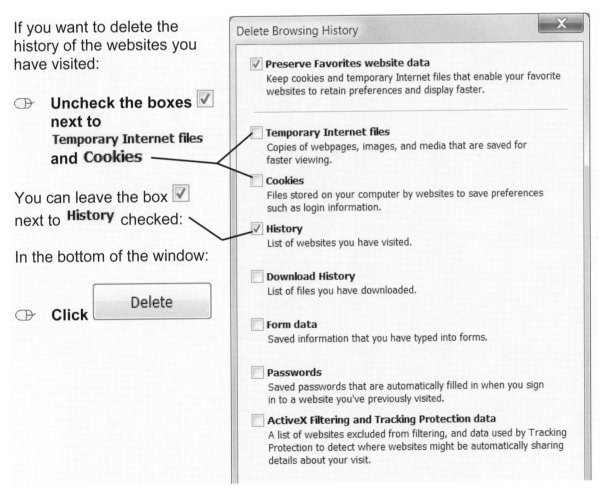

You can also delete all the
stored information at once:

☞ **If necessary, check
the boxes ✓ next to all
the elements**

In the bottom of the window:

☞ **Click** [Delete]

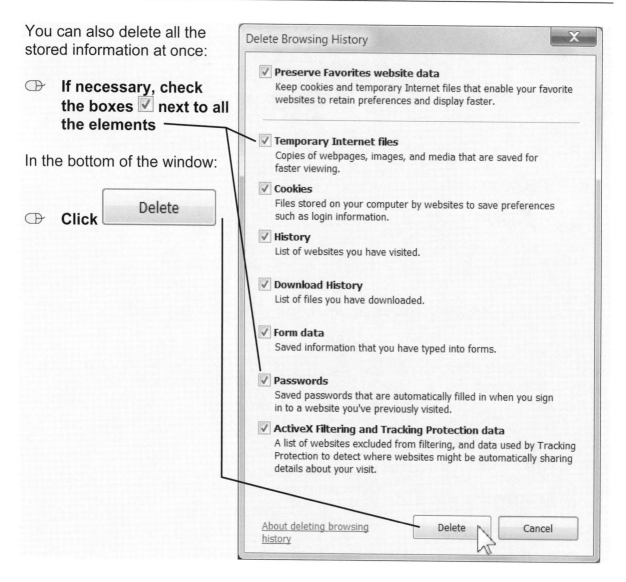

Delete Browsing History   X

✓ **Preserve Favorites website data**
Keep cookies and temporary Internet files that enable your favorite
websites to retain preferences and display faster.

✓ **Temporary Internet files**
Copies of webpages, images, and media that are saved for
faster viewing.

✓ **Cookies**
Files stored on your computer by websites to save preferences
such as login information.

✓ **History**
List of websites you have visited.

✓ **Download History**
List of files you have downloaded.

✓ **Form data**
Saved information that you have typed into forms.

✓ **Passwords**
Saved passwords that are automatically filled in when you sign
in to a website you've previously visited.

✓ **ActiveX Filtering and Tracking Protection data**
A list of websites excluded from filtering, and data used by Tracking
Protection to detect where websites might be automatically sharing
details about your visit.

About deleting browsing
history   [Delete]   [Cancel]

2.2 Set the Number of Days for the History

In the *Internet Options* window there are a number of settings that you can adjust. For example, you can determine how long the web addresses of the websites you visited will be saved in the browsing history. This will prevent you from saving too much information and building up a lot of wasteful files:

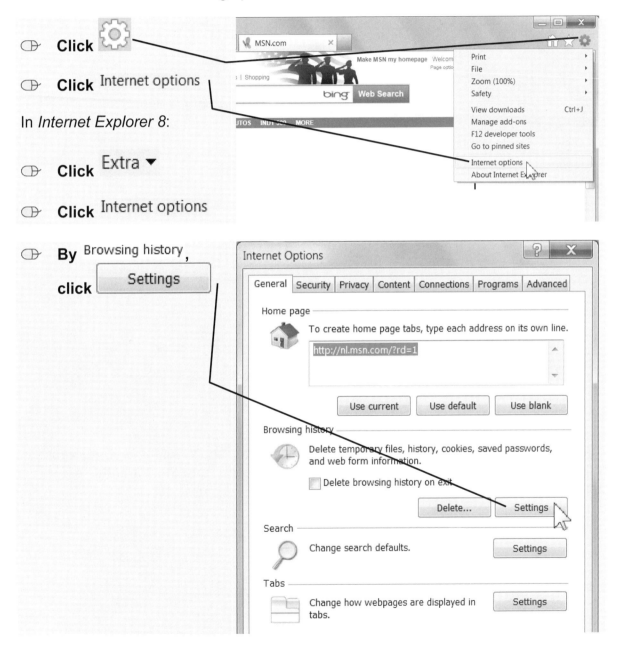

☞ **Click** ⚙

☞ **Click** Internet options

In *Internet Explorer 8*:

☞ **Click** Extra ▼

☞ **Click** Internet options

☞ **By** Browsing history,

click [Settings]

In this example, the list of websites that you have visited is saved for twenty days:

You can use the ⬓ buttons to change this amount.

When you have finished:

☞ **Click** OK

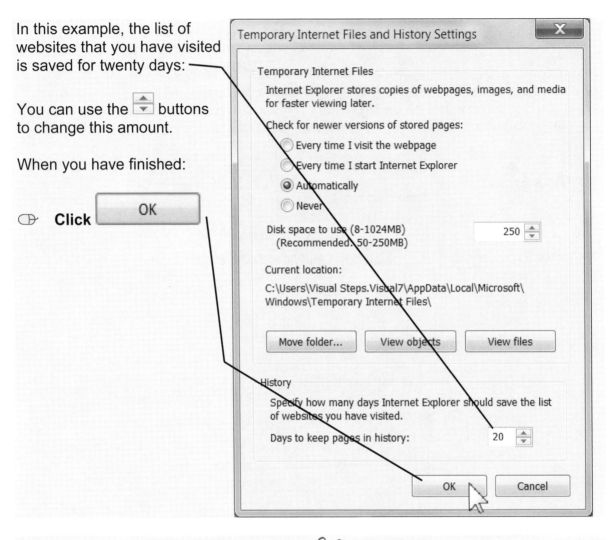

Temporary Internet Files and History Settings   ✕

Temporary Internet Files

Internet Explorer stores copies of webpages, images, and media for faster viewing later.

Check for newer versions of stored pages:

○ Every time I visit the webpage
○ Every time I start Internet Explorer
◉ Automatically
○ Never

Disk space to use (8-1024MB)   250 ⬓
(Recommended 50-250MB)

Current location:

C:\Users\Visual Steps.Visual7\AppData\Local\Microsoft\
Windows\Temporary Internet Files\

[Move folder...]   [View objects]   [View files]

History

Specify how many days Internet Explorer should save the list of websites you have visited.

Days to keep pages in history: 20 ⬓

[OK]   [Cancel]

☞ **Close the *Internet Options* window** 🦶²

After you have cleaned up the history, the folder will be empty. All the web addresses of the sites you have previously visited have been erased from the computer's memory.

💡 Tip

Deleting part of the history
You can also delete individual websites from the history. Here is how you do that:

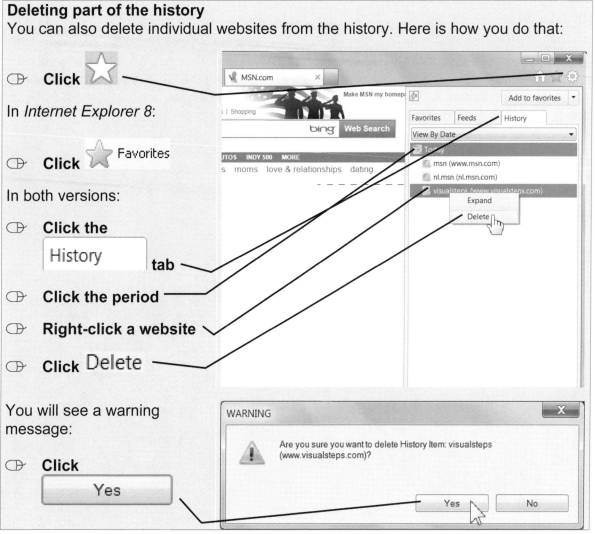

☞ **Click** ☆

In *Internet Explorer 8*:

☞ **Click** ☆ Favorites

In both versions:

☞ **Click the**
  History **tab**

☞ **Click the period**

☞ **Right-click a website**

☞ **Click** Delete

You will see a warning message:

☞ **Click**
  Yes

2.3 Deleting a Program

After using your computer for a while, you may find that you have accumulated a lot of programs you hardly ever use. To free up space you can delete these programs. To properly delete a program, you should not just delete the program file, but you need to uninstall the program. This will make sure that all the program's components will be completely removed from your computer's hard drive.
This is how you delete a program in *Windows 7* and *Vista*:

☞ **Click** 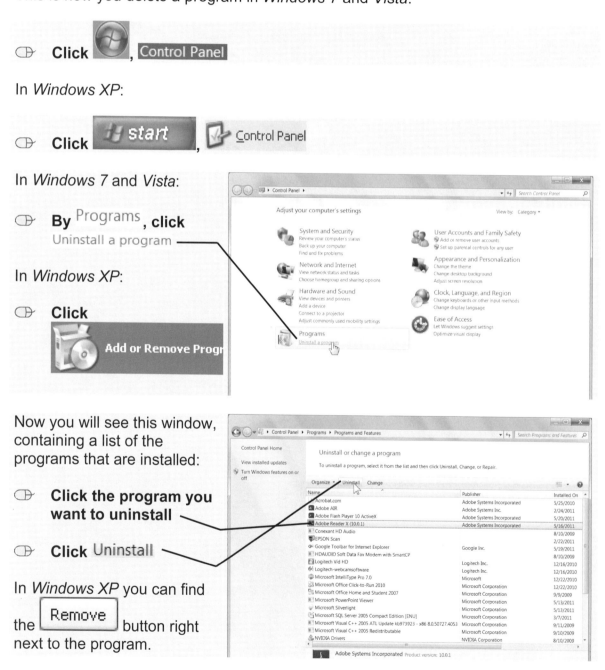 , Control Panel

In *Windows XP*:

☞ **Click** start , Control Panel

In *Windows 7* and *Vista*:

☞ **By** Programs **, click** Uninstall a program

In *Windows XP*:

☞ **Click**
Add or Remove Progr

Now you will see this window, containing a list of the programs that are installed:

☞ **Click the program you want to uninstall**

☞ **Click** Uninstall

In *Windows XP* you can find the Remove button right next to the program.

☞ **If necessary, give permission to continue**

⬎ **Please note:**

The list of programs also contains auxiliary programs, which are needed for the execution of other programs. Most likely, you will not recognize the names of these auxiliary programs. That is why you should only delete the programs that you know. If you are not sure, check if the publisher of the program is a well-known company, and if you have installed other programs made by the same company.

⬡ **Click**
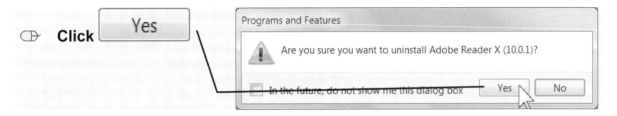

Now the program will be removed from the computer.

⬎ **Please note:**

When you are uninstalling programs, some of the programs will ask you if you just wish to uninstall specific components. Then you will see additional windows.

☞ **Follow the operations in the windows**

☞ **Close the window** ✂²

💡 **Tip**

Uninstall a program from the Start menu
The programs listed in the Start menu will often contain an uninstall option as well. You can also use this option to uninstall a program:

⬡ **Click the uninstall option for the desired program**

2.4 Cleaning Up Your Computer in Windows 7

Your computer's hard drive contains lots of information that is stored on a temporary basis. These temporary files can slow down your computer. These files might be the web pages you have visited, temporary files created by specific programs, safety copies, etcetera. By doing a regular clean up, you will free up extra space on the hard drive and your computer will operate faster.

This is how you clean up your hard drive:

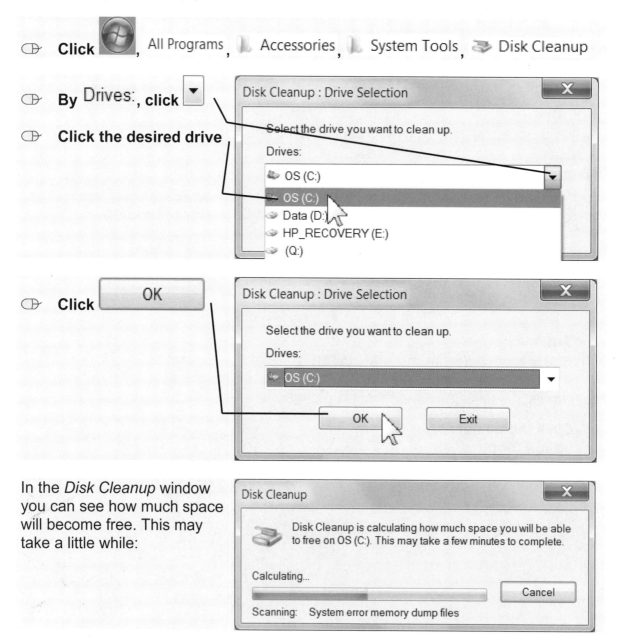

☞ **Click** 🪟, All Programs , ⬛ Accessories , ⬛ System Tools , 📚 Disk Cleanup

☞ **By** Drives: **, click** ▼

☞ **Click the desired drive**

☞ **Click** OK

In the *Disk Cleanup* window you can see how much space will become free. This may take a little while:

Here you see a list of files that can be deleted. When you click an item, you will see a description of it in the window: —————

Normally, you can delete everything that appears on this list. If you do not want to do this, then uncheck the boxes ☑ next to the items you do not wish to remove: ⟍

In this example, the total amount of disk space that will become free is 101 MB.

By clicking [OK] you will only delete the files that belong to your own user account.

☞ **Click**

[🛡 Clean up system files] ⟋

Disk Cleanup for OS (C:)

Disk Cleanup

You can use Disk Cleanup to free up to 101 MB of disk space on OS (C:).

Files to delete:

☐ 📄 Offline webpages	14.1 KB	▲
☑ 🗑 Recycle Bin	2.57 KB	
☑ Temporary files	73.7 MB	≡
☑ Thumbnails	3.00 MB	
☑ System archived Windows Error Reporting ...	4.20 KB	▼

Total amount of disk space you gain: 101 MB

Description

Downloaded Program Files are ActiveX controls and Java applets downloaded automatically from the Internet when you view certain pages. They are temporarily stored in the Downloaded Program Files folder on your hard disk.

[🛡 Clean up system files]   [View Files]

How does Disk Cleanup work?

[OK]   [Cancel]

☞ **If necessary, give permission to continue**

Now you will see the *Disk Cleanup* window again. The difference is, in this case you are going to let *Disk Cleanup* check the files of all the user accounts on the computer:

☞ **By** Drives:**, click** ▼

☞ **Click the desired drive**

Disk Cleanup : Drive Selection

Select the drive you want to clean up.

Drives:

[💾 OS (C:)] ▼

OS (C:)
💿 Data (D:)
💿 HP_RECOVERY (E:)
💿 (Q:)

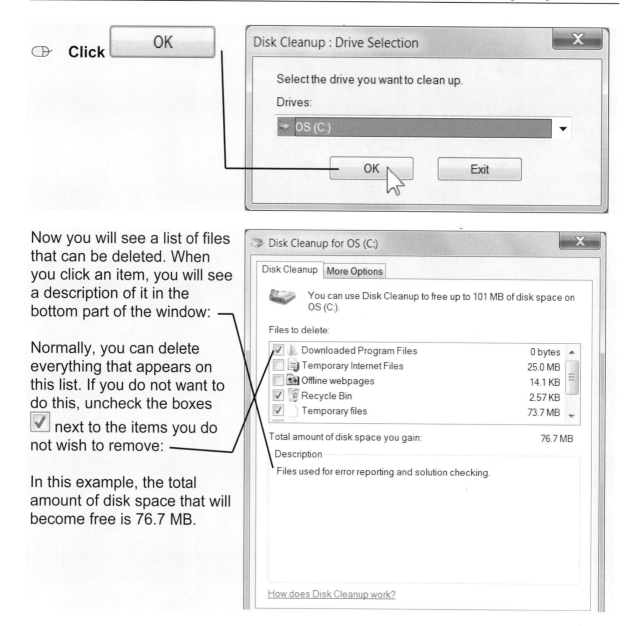

☞ **Click** [OK]

Now you will see a list of files that can be deleted. When you click an item, you will see a description of it in the bottom part of the window: ⌐

Normally, you can delete everything that appears on this list. If you do not want to do this, uncheck the boxes ✓ next to the items you do not wish to remove: ⌐

In this example, the total amount of disk space that will become free is 76.7 MB.

Sometimes, you will see other program files and system files that can be deleted as well. You can delete these files in the following window:

☞ **Click the**
    [More Options] **tab**

☞ **By** Programs and Features,
    click [Clean up...]

Now you will see all the programs that are installed on your computer:

You can read more about deleting programs in *section 2.3 Deleting a Program*.

☞ **Click** ⬛

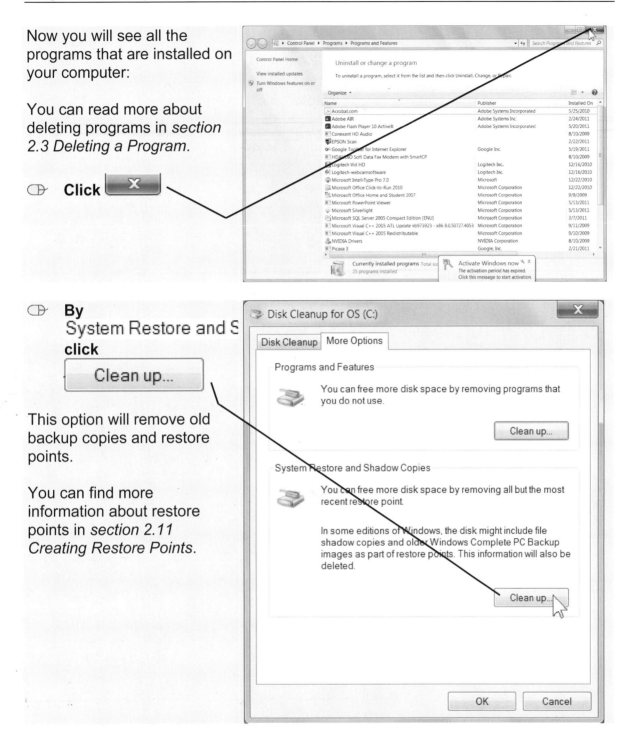

☞ **By System Restore and S̶ click**

Clean up...

This option will remove old backup copies and restore points.

You can find more information about restore points in *section 2.11 Creating Restore Points*.

☞ **Click** Delete

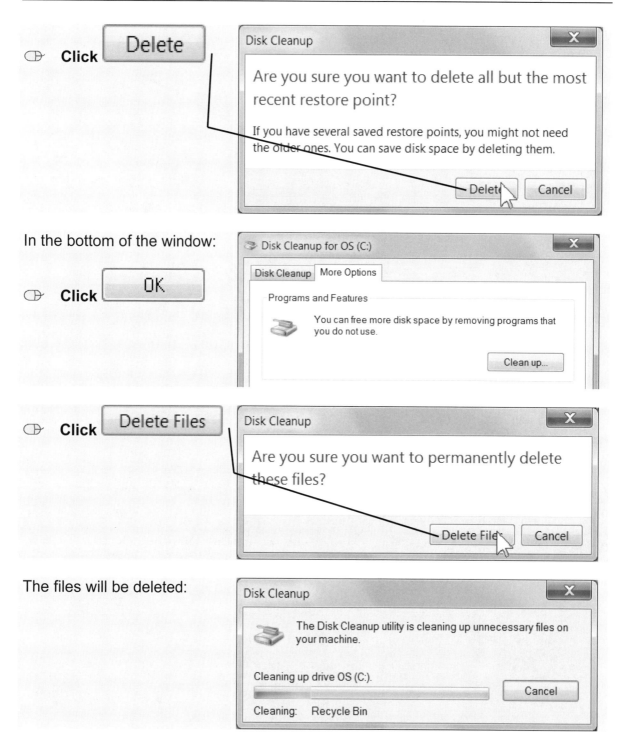

In the bottom of the window:

☞ **Click** OK

☞ **Click** Delete Files

The files will be deleted:

Disk Cleanup has now deleted the files you selected.

2.5 Cleaning Up Your Computer in Windows Vista and XP

Your computer's hard drive contains lots of information that is stored on a temporary basis. These temporary files can slow down your computer. These files might be the web pages you have visited, temporary files created by specific programs, safety copies, etcetera. By doing a regular clean up, you will free up extra space on the hard drive and your computer will operate faster.

This is how you clean up your hard drive:

In *Windows Vista*:

☞ **Click** ⊕ , All Programs , Accessories , System Tools , Disk Cleanup

In *Windows XP*:

☞ **Click** start , All Programs , Accessories , System Tools , Disk Cleanup

☞ **Click**
    Files from all users on th

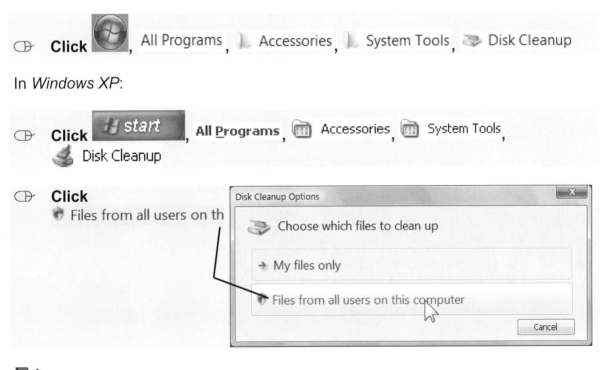

⤷ Please note:

If your computer is also used by other people, then select My files only. Otherwise, you may delete files owned by other users. In this case, you will not free up as much space as you would by deleting files used by others.

☞ **If necessary, give permission to continue**

☞ **If necessary, by**

Drives:**, click** ▼

☞ **Click the desired drive**

☞ **If necessary, click**

    OK

Disk Cleanup will examine
the disk:

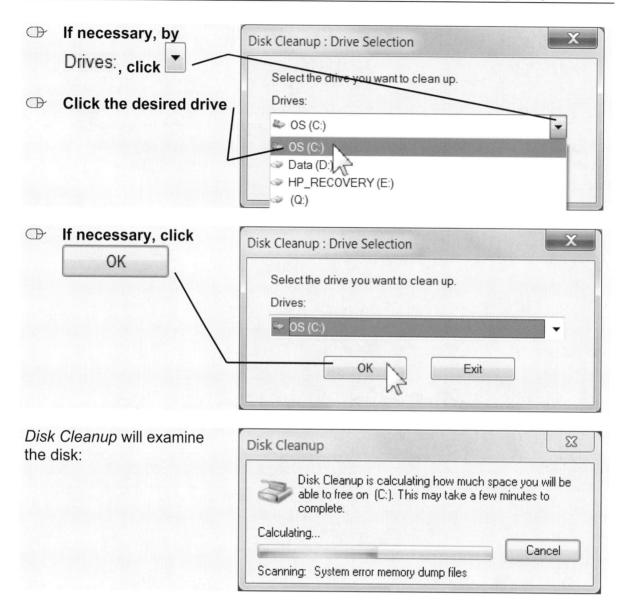

Here you will see a list of files that can be deleted. When you click an item, you will see a description in the bottom of the window: ———

Normally you can delete all of the items on this list. If you do not want to do this, then uncheck the boxes ☑ next to the items you do not wish to remove: ———

In this example, the total amount of disk space that will become free is 17.5 MB.

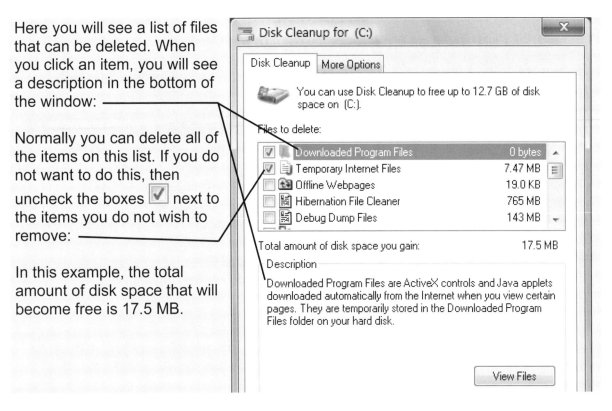

Sometimes, you can also delete other program files and system files. This is how you do that:

☞ **Click the** More Options **tab**

In *Windows Vista*:

☞ **By** Programs and Features, **click** Clean up...

In *Windows XP*:

☞ **By** Installed programs, **click** Clean up...

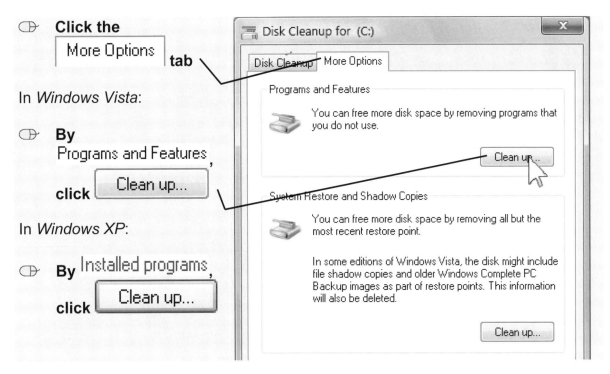

HELP! I do not see the | More Options | **tab**

If you have selected the My files only tab, the | More Options | tab will not be present. If that is the case, continue on page 96.

You will see all the programs that are installed on your computer:

You can read more about deleting programs in *section 2.3 Deleting a Program*.

➲ **Click** [X]

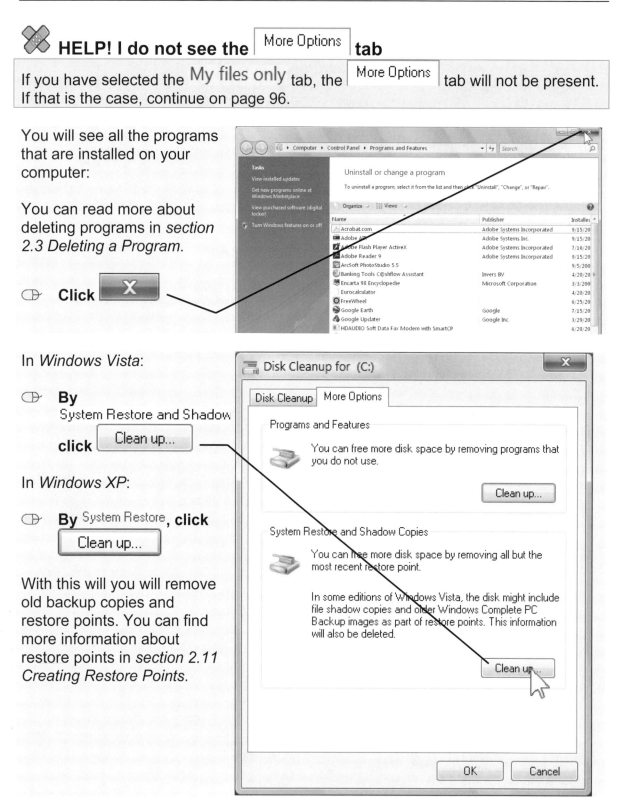

In *Windows Vista*:

➲ **By** System Restore and Shadow **click** [Clean up...]

In *Windows XP*:

➲ **By** System Restore, **click** [Clean up...]

With this will you will remove old backup copies and restore points. You can find more information about restore points in *section 2.11 Creating Restore Points*.

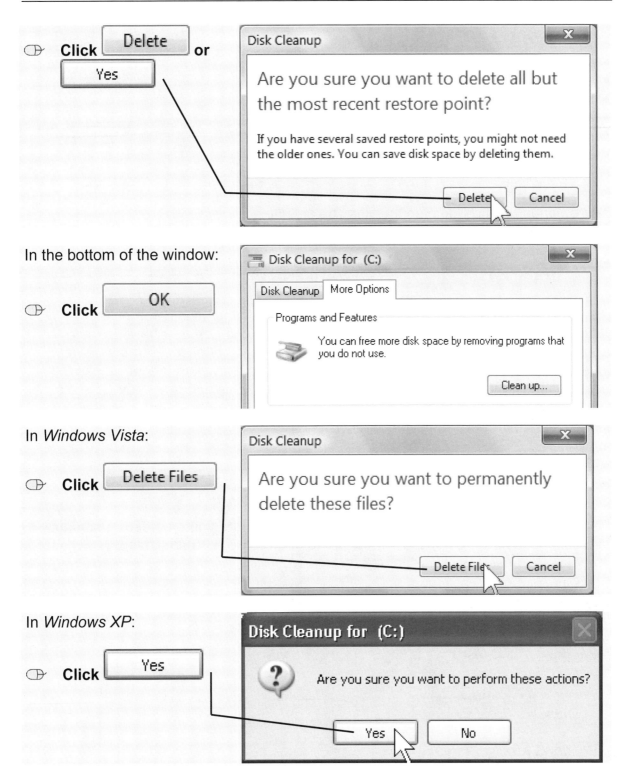

⊕ **Click** Delete **or**

Yes

In the bottom of the window:

⊕ **Click** OK

In *Windows Vista*:

⊕ **Click** Delete Files

In *Windows XP*:

⊕ **Click** Yes

Now the files will be deleted:

Disk Cleanup

The Disk Cleanup utility is cleaning up unnecessary files on your machine.

Cleaning up drive (C:).

Cleaning: Thumbnails

Cancel

Disk Cleanup has now deleted the files you selected.

2.6 Check Disk

The hard drive is one of the few moving mechanical elements in a computer. Because mechanical parts can wear down, you should check your hard drive on a regular basis. *Windows* uses the *Check Disk* function to check the surface of the drive and mark possible damaged sectors. These sectors will no longer be used. If these sectors contain data, *Check Disk* will try to save this data and move it to a safe location. This will result in greater reliability, as well as greater speed, because it takes a longer time to retrieve data from damaged parts of the hard drive.

Please note:

Check Disk is also called *Error-checking*.

It is recommended to run the *Check Disk* operation before you do a defragmentation. If you do this, *Windows* will know which parts of the drive are unreliable and will not store data to these sectors when defragmenting.

In *Windows*, you can use the (*My*) *Computer* option to check your computer for errors:

In *Windows 7* and *Vista*:

⊕ **Click** , Computer

In *Windows XP*:

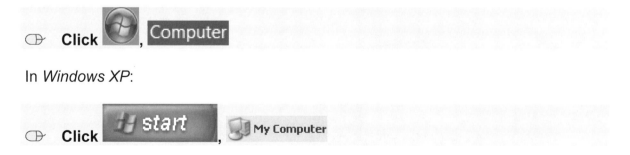

⊕ **Click** start , My Computer

You will see the (*My*)
Computer window:

☞ **Right-click the drive
you want to check**

☞ **Click** Properties

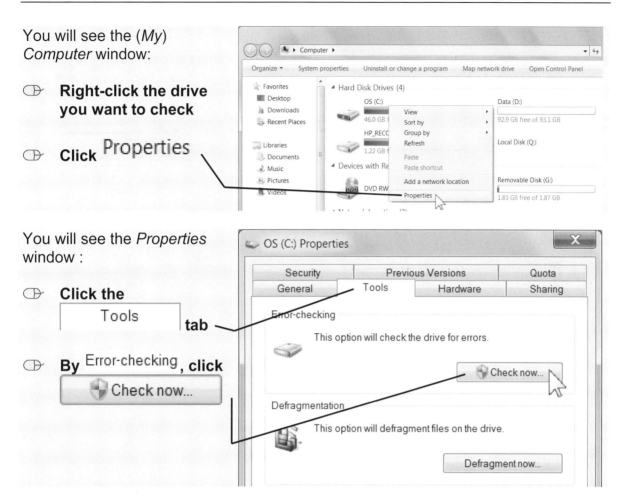

You will see the *Properties*
window :

☞ **Click the**

Tools **tab**

☞ **By** Error-checking**, click**

Check now...

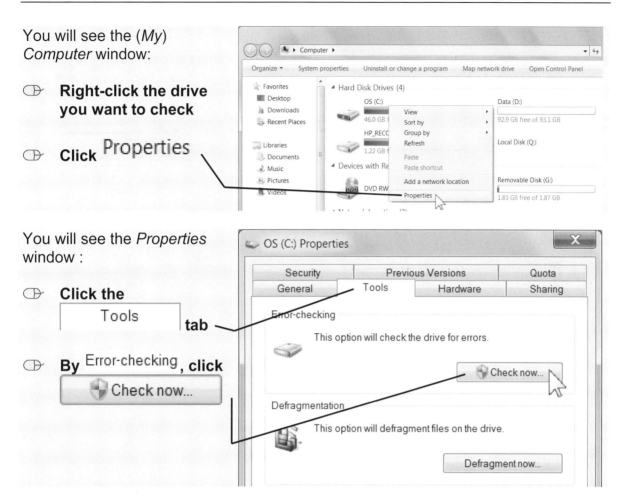

☞ **If necessary, give permission to continue**

You will see this window:

☞ **If necessary, check
the box ☑ by**
Automatically fix file system

☞ **If necessary, check
the box ☑ by**
Scan for and attempt re

☞ **Click** Start

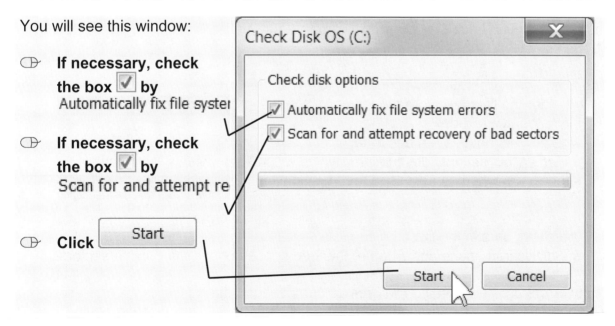

The `Automatically fix file system errors` option will only check if all the data is still located in the correct place on the drive. This check will be executed quite quickly. The `Scan for and attempt recovery of bad sectors` option will check the technical reliability of the actual disk. This process will take up more time.

➥ **Please note:**

Check Disk may take several hours, if you have a large hard drive. If you wish to postpone the check, click [Cancel] in the following window.

☞ **Close all windows** ✍² **and restart the computer**

➥ **Please note:**

If you still want to postpone the *Check Disk* operation after the restart, then press a key, when prompted to do so after the restart. If you do not do anything after the restart, then the *Check Disk* operation will start automatically. You will not be able to abort this action.

The *Check Disk* operation will check the following things:
- whether the files are stored in the correct location, that is to say, the location indicated by the index;
- whether the indexes are accurate;
- the so-called 'security descriptions' which will indicate who is the owner of a specific file, who has access to the file and which operations are allowed with this file;
- the file data, that is, the contents of the file. The contents will be checked against the check data in the file;
- the disk's free space and whether this free space contains unreliable sectors.

If any errors are detected, you will see error messages during the check operation. When the *Check Disk* operation has finished, *Windows* will start working again.

HELP! Errors are found

Usually, there is no need for concern when *Check Disk* detects errors on your hard drive. In the course of time, most hard drives will show signs of wear and the magnetic surface will contract some minor damage.

By regularly checking your computer with *Check Disk,* you will often be able to save the data in damaged sectors. But if you wait too long, you will detect ever more errors and your computer will start slowing down. There is also a greater chance of losing data.

Does the number of errors increase with each check? Then this might indicate that your hard drive needs to be replaced.

2.7 Defragmenting Your Computer in Windows 7

In the course of time, the files on your computer will become fragmented and blank spaces will arise. This is due to the fact that you regularly delete files. The blank spaces are filled again when you save other files or install new programs. To get your computer to operate more efficiently, you will need to re-organize all existing files, using the *Disk Defragmenter* function. The files will then be stored on your computer in an efficient manner, which will ensure that you can access them as quick as possible.

Please note:

To use *Disk Defragmenter* your hard drive needs to have at least 15% free space.

Please note:

Depending on the size of your hard drive and the degree of fragmentation, the defragmentation process may take as little time as just a few minutes. But if there is a lot of fragmentation, it can take up to a few hours.

This is how to defragment your computer:

⊕ **Click** , All Programs , Accessories , System Tools , Disk Cleanup , Disk Defragmenter

You will see the *Disk Defragmenter* window:

☞ **Click the drive you want to defragment**

☞ **Click**

Defragment disk

The drive will be analyzed:

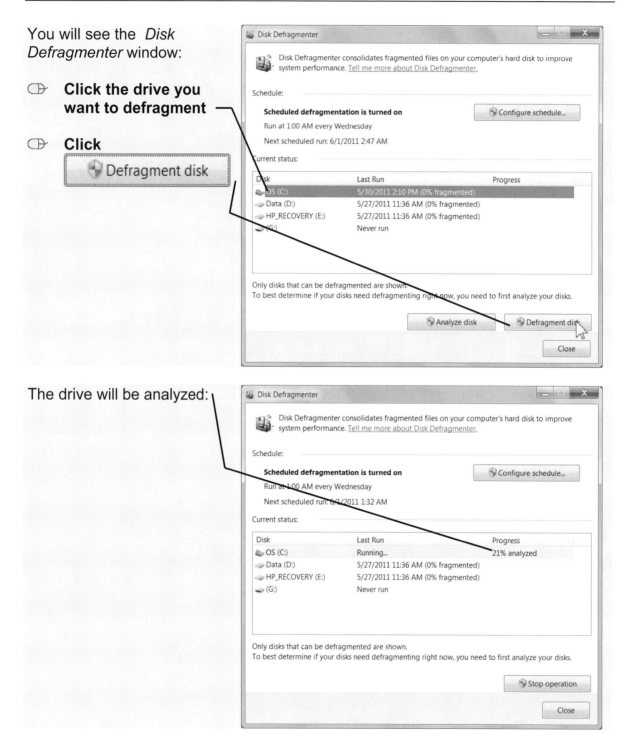

If no problems are detected, defragmentation starts right away. Depending on the size of the drive and the degree of fragmentation, it may take a while:

The defragmentation process starts: ⎯⎯⎯⎯

During the defragmentation process you should not turn your computer off. You can continue working as usual.

Disk Defragmenter		— □ X

Disk Defragmenter consolidates fragmented files on your computer's hard disk to improve system performance. Tell me more about Disk Defragmenter.

Schedule:

Scheduled defragmentation is turned on   [Configure schedule...]

Run at 1:00 AM every Wednesday

Next scheduled run: 6/1/2011 1:32 AM

Current status:

Disk	Last Run	Progress
OS (C:)	Running...	Pass 1: 3% relocated
Data (D:)	5/27/2011 11:36 AM (0% fragmented)	
HP_RECOVERY (E:)	5/27/2011 11:36 AM (0% fragmented)	
(G:)	Never run	

Only disks that can be defragmented are shown.
To best determine if your disks need defragmenting right now, you need to first analyze your disks.

[Stop operation]

[Close]

If the defragmentation was successful, the result will be that 0% of the drive is fragmented: ⎯⎯⎯⎯

🖰 **Click** [Close]

Disk Defragmenter		— □ X

Disk Defragmenter consolidates fragmented files on your computer's hard disk to improve system performance. Tell me more about Disk Defragmenter.

Schedule:

Scheduled defragmentation is turned on   [Configure schedule...]

Run at 1:00 AM every Wednesday

Next scheduled run: 6/1/2011 1:32 AM

Current status:

Disk	Last Run	Progress
OS (C:)	5/30/2011 3:08 PM (0% fragmented)	
Data (D:)	5/27/2011 11:36 AM (0% fragmented)	
HP_RECOVERY (E:)	5/27/2011 11:36 AM (0% fragmented)	
(G:)	Never run	

Only disks that can be defragmented are shown.
To best determine if your disks need defragmenting right now, you need to first analyze your disks.

[Analyze disk]   [Defragment disk]

[Close]

☼ **Tip**

Automatic defragmenter in Windows 7

If you use your computer very often, it is recommended that you set the *Disk Defragmenter* to perform an automatic defragmentation on a regular basis. In the *Disk Defragmenter* window:

☞ **Click** 🛡 Configure schedule...

☞ **Select the desired frequency**

☞ **Click** OK

Disk Defragmenter: Modify Schedule ✕

Disk defragmenter schedule configuration:

☑ Run on a schedule (recommended)

Frequency: Monthly ▾

Day: 1 ▾

Time: 1:00 AM ▾

Disks: Select disks...

OK   Cancel

2.8 Defragmenting Your Computer in Windows Vista

In the course of time, the files on your computer will become fragmented and blank spaces will arise. This is due to the fact that you regularly delete files. The blank spaces are filled again when you save other files or install new programs. To get your computer to operate more efficiently, you will need to re-organize all existing files, using the *Disk Defragmenter* function. The files will then be stored on your computer in an efficient manner, which will ensure that you can access them as quick as possible.

➥ **Please note:**

To use *Disk Defragmenter* your hard drive needs to have at least 15% free space.

Please note:

Depending on the size of your hard drive and the degree of fragmentation, the defragmentation process may take as little time as just a few minutes. But if there is a lot of fragmentation, it can take up to a few hours.

This is how to defragment your computer:

Click , All Programs , Accessories , System Tools , Disk Cleanup ,

Disk Defragmenter

☞ **If necessary, give permission to continue**

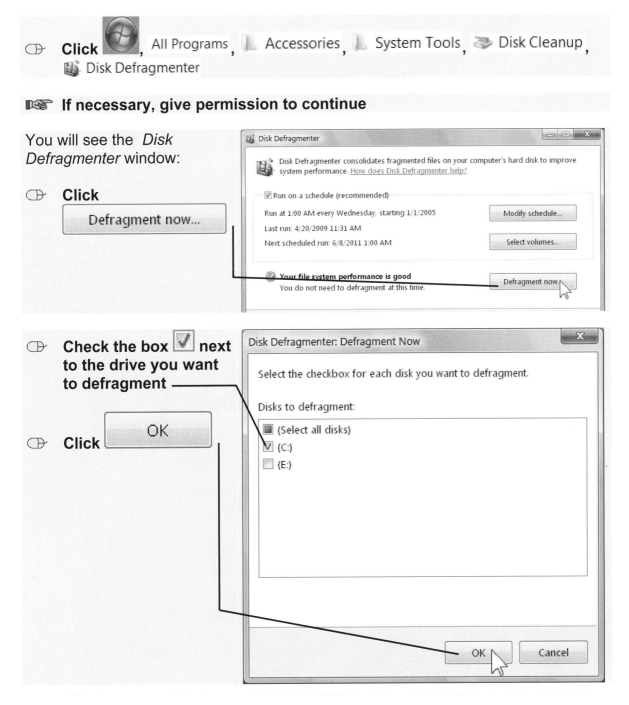

You will see the *Disk Defragmenter* window:

Click

Defragment now...

Check the box ✓ **next to the drive you want to defragment** ——

Click OK

The defragmentation process starts:

During the defragmentation process you should not turn your computer off. You can continue working as usual.

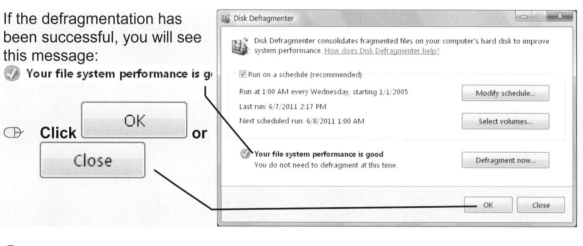

If the defragmentation has been successful, you will see this message:

✓ **Your file system performance is g**

⊕ **Click** [OK] **or**

[Close]

Tip

Automatic defragmentation
If you use your computer very often, it is recommended that you let the *Disk Defragmenter* perform the defragmentation automatically.

⊕ **Check the box ☑ next to**
Run on a schedule (recommen

☞ **Set the time at**
[Modify schedule...]

If you use multiple drives:

☞ **Select these drives at**
[Select volumes...]

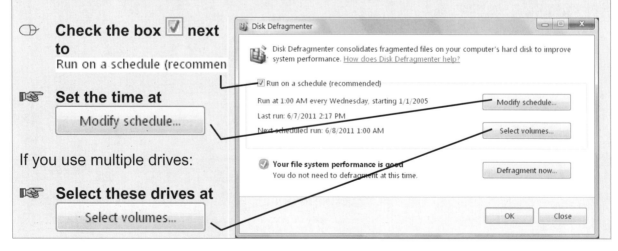

2.9 Defragmenting Your Computer in Windows XP

In the course of time, the files on your computer will become fragmented and blank spaces will arise. This is due to the fact that you regularly delete files. The blank spaces are filled again when you save other files or install new programs. To get your computer to operate more efficiently, you will need to re-organize all existing files, using the *Disk Defragmenter* function. The files will then be stored on your computer in an efficient manner, which will ensure that you can access them as quick as possible.

➥ **Please note:**

To use *Disk Defragmenter* your hard drive needs to have at least 15% free space.

➥ **Please note:**

Depending on the size of your hard drive and the degree of fragmentation, the defragmentation process may take as little time as just a few minutes. But if there is a lot of fragmentation, it can take up to a few hours.

This is how to defragment your computer:

☞ **Click** `start`, **All Programs**, Accessories, System Tools, Disk Defragmenter

You will see the *Disk Defragmenter* window:

☞ **Click the drive (Volume) you want to defragment**

First, the drive will be analyzed:

☞ **Click** Analyze

This analysis will let you know the amount of defragmentation (if any) needed. In this example we will select the *Defragment* option anyways, even if the system indicates that defragmenting is not necessary.

When the analysis is done, you will see this window:

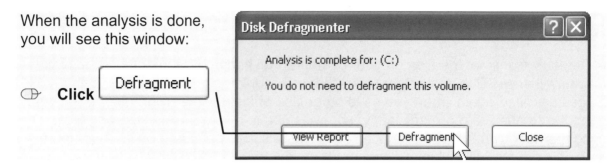

⊕ **Click** | Defragment |

Depending on the size of the disk and the degree of fragmentation, this may take a while:

The defragmentation process starts:

During the defragmentation process you should not turn your computer off. You can continue working as usual.

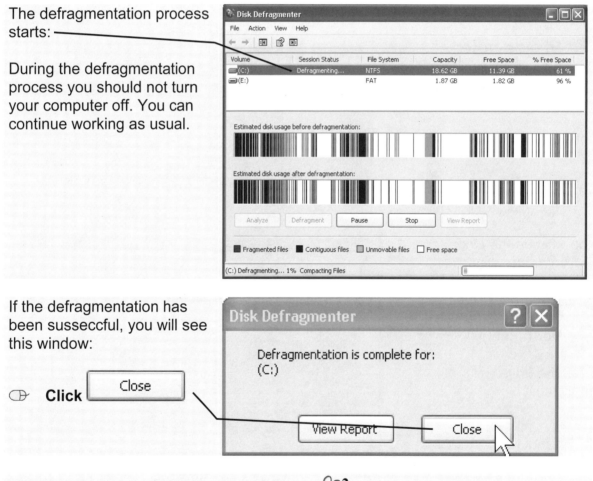

If the defragmentation has been susseccful, you will see this window:

⊕ **Click** | Close |

☞ **Close the *Disk Defragmenter* window** ⸿²

2.10 System Restore

The *System Restore* program is another *Windows* component. This program monitors changes in the operating system and in certain applications. After you have used your computer for a certain amount of time, *Windows* will create restore points automatically. But you can also create restore points yourself, whenever you want. A good example, for instance, could be just before introducing a major change to your computer. These restore pints enable you to restore the system to an earlier state.

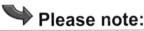 **Please note:**

The *System Restore* program only monitors the changes in the operating system and some specific application files. Restoring a previous system status will not affect your personal data files. Your files, such as text files, e-mail messages, photos, etcetera., will not be changed. This means you cannot use *System Restore* to undo the deleting of a document, an e-mail message or a photo.

Reverting to a restore point is a good idea if your computer malfunctions all of a sudden. This may be the case after you have installed new software or after you have deleted or moved certain files. You can try to solve the problems by restoring the system to a previously created restore point. You will need to select a restore point from a period where you did not yet experience any problem.

2.11 Creating Restore Points

Windows creates restore points on a daily basis and also at important occasions, for instance when you install new programs or devices. If you wish, you can also create your own restore points at crucial moments. This is how you do that:

In *Windows 7* and *Vista*:

Click , Control Panel

Click System and Security **or** System and Maintenance

Click System

☞ **Click**
Advanced system settin

☞ **If necessary, give permission to continue**

The *System Properties* window will be opened:

☞ **Click the**
| System Protection |
tab

You can only create restore
points for drives that have
system protection turned on.
Usually that will only be the
C: drive where the *Windows*
program has been installed:

☞ **Click**
| Create... |

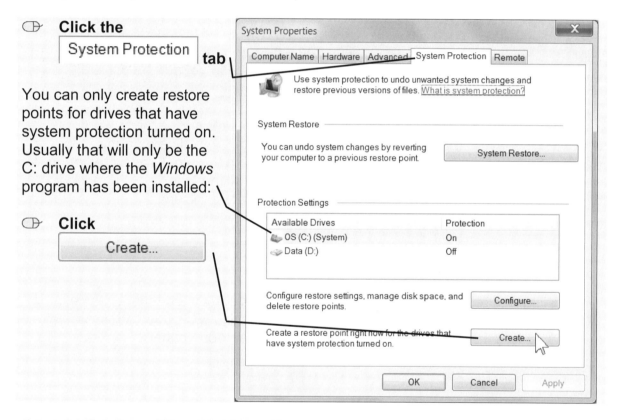

☞ **Continue with the *Create a restore point* window on page 109**

In *Windows XP*:

☞ **Click**

Click
`Undo changes to your computer`

You will see the *System Restore* window:

Click the radio button ◉ **by**
Create a restore point

Click `Next >`

⌨ **Type a name for the restore point**

Click `Create`

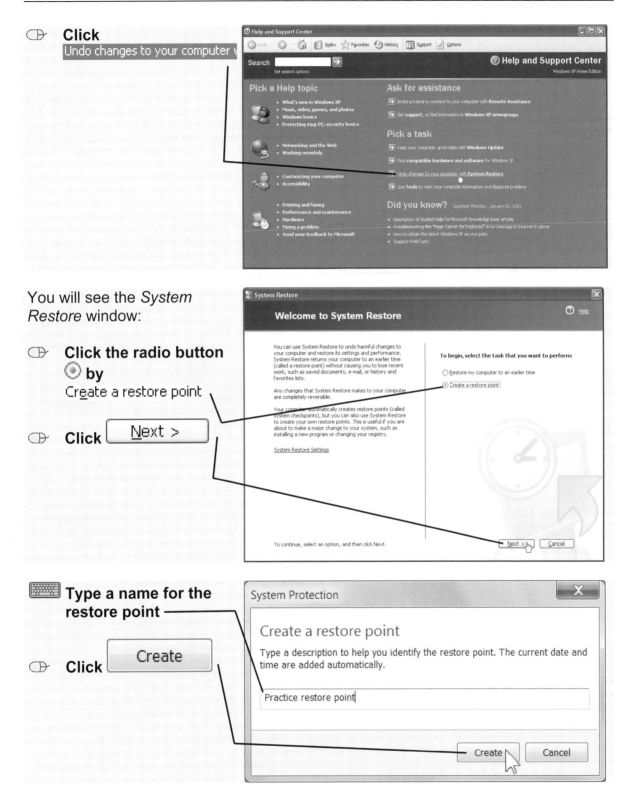

In *Windows 7* and *Vista* you may see this window while you are creating a restore point:

In *Windows 7* and *Vista*, you will see the following window when the restore point has been created:

In *Windows XP*, you will see this window when the restore point has been created:

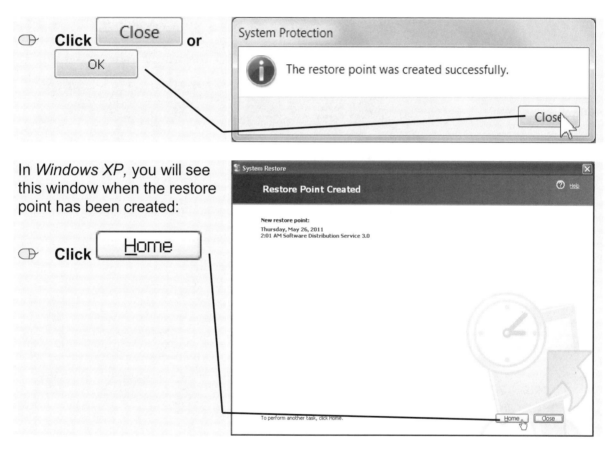

Next you will see the *System Properties* window again.

2.12 Restoring the System to an Earlier Point in Windows 7 and Vista

In the *System Properties* window you can use *System Restore* to revert to a previous restore point.

Please note:

Only execute the operations in this section if you are actually experiencing problems with your computer. If you do not have any problems, then just read through this section.

Please note:

Using *System Restore* will cause your computer to restart. It is recommended to close all programs and save all your work, before starting the *System Restore* process.

☞ **If necessary, open the *System Properties* window** 🐾[5]

In the *System Properties* window:

☞ **Click**

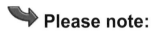

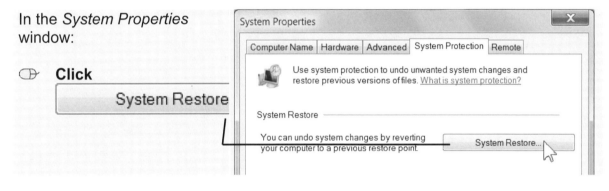

💡 Tip

Another way to start System Restore
In *Windows 7*, you can also start *System Restore* in the following manner:

☞ **Open the *Control Panel*** 🐾[4]

☞ **Click** System and Security

☞ **By** Action Center**, click** Restore your computer to an earlier time

The *Recovery* window will be opened:

Click [Open System Restore]

Please note: if you do not see this window here, you will see it in the next screen shot.

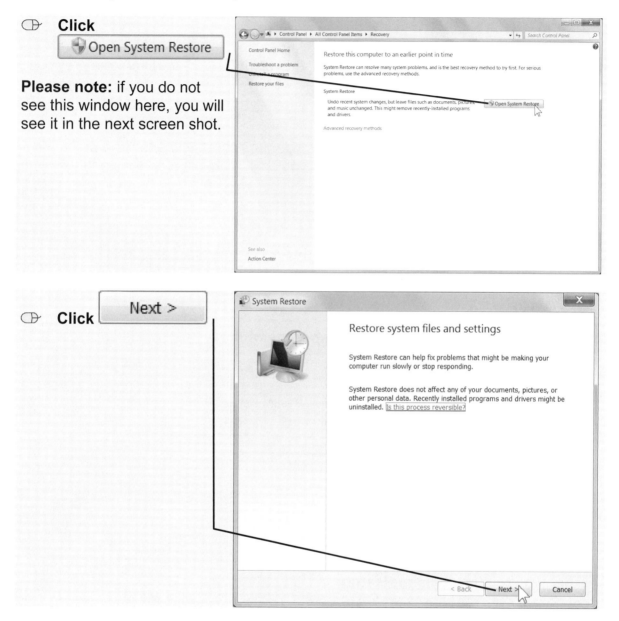

Click [Next >]

You may also see this window:

👉 **Click the radio button** ⦿ **by**
Choose a different restore ¡

👉 **Click** [Next >]

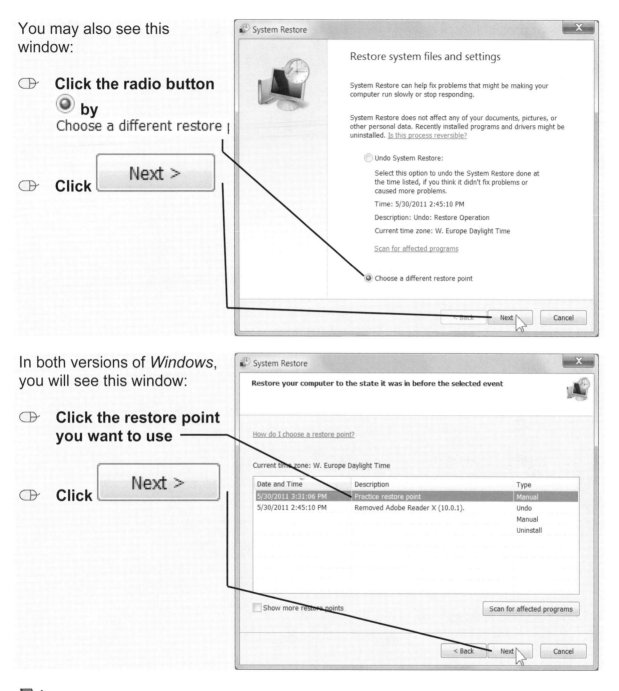

In both versions of *Windows*, you will see this window:

👉 **Click the restore point you want to use**

👉 **Click** [Next >]

➥ Please note:

By default, the restore points for the previous five days will be displayed. If your problem has occurred at an earlier stage, for instance a week ago, when you installed a new printer, you can check the box ☑ next to Show more restore points. Then you will be able to see older restore points.

If you have multiple hard drives, you may see the *Confirm disk to restore* window:

Click Next >

In this example, the practice restore point is created for the C: drive: ———

Click Finish

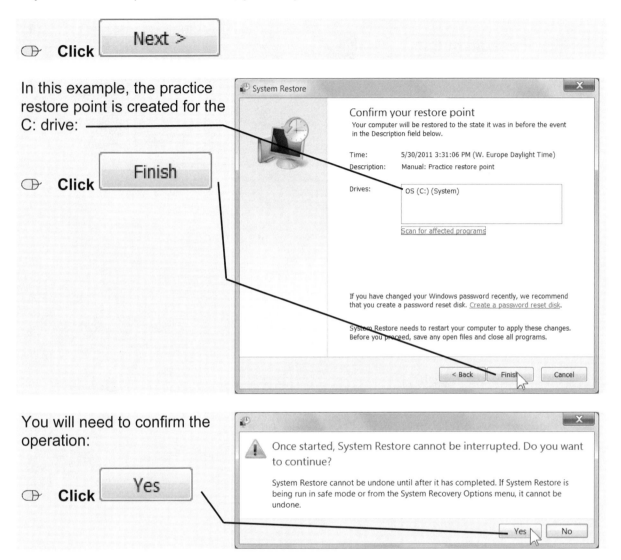

You will need to confirm the operation:

Click Yes

System Restore will start restoring the system files.

When *System Restore* has finished, *Windows* will close and then restart. When your desktop appears again, you will see this message:

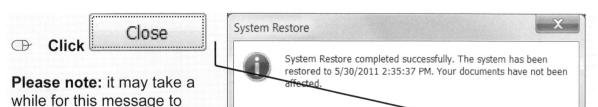

Now the computer has been restored to a previous state. There is a good chance of the problem being solved. If the problem has not been solved, you can let an expert or an experienced user take a look at your computer. But you can also search for some additional information on the Internet.

2.13 Restoring the System to an Earlier Point in Windows XP

In the *System Restore* window you can restore the system to a restore point.

⤵ Please note:

Only execute the operations in this section if you are actually experiencing problems with your computer. If you do not have any problems, then just read through this section.

⤵ Please note:

Using *System Restore* will cause your computer to restart. It is recommended to close all programs and save all your work, before starting the *System Restore* process.

☞ **If necessary, open the *System Restore* window** ⑧⑧⁵

In the *System Restore* window:

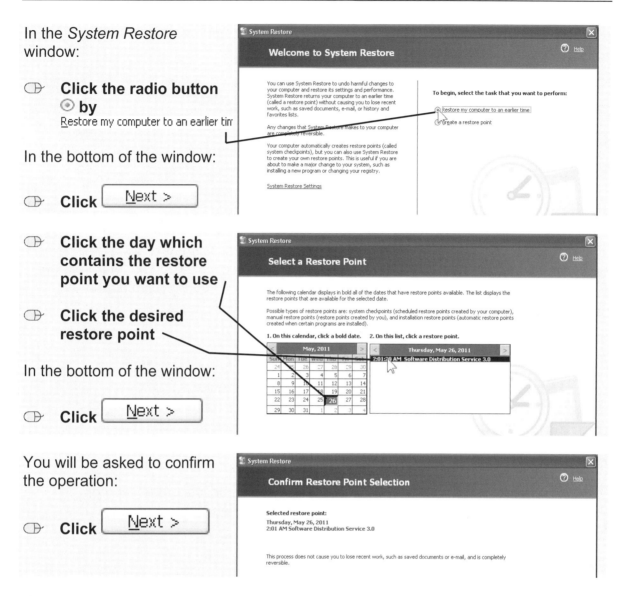

⊕ **Click the radio button ⊙ by**
R̲estore my computer to an earlier tin

In the bottom of the window:

⊕ **Click** Ne̲xt >

⊕ **Click the day which contains the restore point you want to use**

⊕ **Click the desired restore point**

In the bottom of the window:

⊕ **Click** Ne̲xt >

You will be asked to confirm the operation:

⊕ **Click** Ne̲xt >

System Restore will start restoring the system files.

When *System Restore* has finished, *Windows XP* will close and then restart. When the desktop appears again, you will see a message that the system has been restored.

⊕ **Click** OK

Now the computer has been restored to a previous state. There is a good chance of the problem being solved. If the problem has not been solved, you can let an expert or an experienced user take a look at your computer. But you can also search for some additional information on the Internet.

2.14 Background Information

Dictionary	
Browser history	The traces you leave behind while surfing the Internet. In *Internet Explorer*, the browser history consists of temporary internet files, cookies, history, data from forms and passwords.
Cookies	Cookies are small text files that websites store on your computer containing information about you and your preferences.
Disk cleanup	If you want to reduce the number of unused or unnecessary files on your computer, to free up space and speed up your computer, you can use *Disk Cleanup*. This function will delete temporary files and delete the files in the *Recycle* Bin, as well as several system files and other files that you no longer need.
Disk defragmenter	Due to fragmentation, the computer has to work harder, which slows it down. The *Disk Defragmenter* will reorganize the data more efficiently and your computer will work faster.
Form data	Information you have entered in forms on the websites you visited.
History	A list of all the websites you visited.
Restore point	The state of the computer at an earlier point in time, which can be restored with the *System Restore* function.
Temporary Internet files	Web pages that you have visited for the first time using your browser will be stored in a folder containing temporary internet files. This allows pages that you have previously visited, or regularly visit, display much faster. That is because *Internet Explorer* opens these pages from the stored version on your computer.
Uninstall	Undo the installation of a program by deleting the program files from the computer.

Source: Windows Help and Support

Disk fragmentation

When you store a file on your computer, it is not be stored in a single location. Depending on the size of the file, it will be divided into small parts (fragments) and stored in different sections on the hard drive. All the fragments together will make up the file. This method is used in order to quickly save and read files. Usually, a hard drive consists of multiple disks, put together in one casing; each side of such a disk contains its own read/write head. You will not notice this, because *Windows* regards this as a single disk drive, referred to as C or D. If you were to save or open a file that would be stored in a single location, that particular read/write head would be very busy, while the rest of the heads would be idle. With the method described above, the work is distributed among all the heads. *Windows* uses tables to keep track of all the fragments, and to record how the various fragments need to be connected.

Whenever you save, modify, or delete files, the hard drive becomes more and more fragmented in due course. The changes you save to a file are often stored in a different location than the original file. After a while, the file as well as the hard drive becomes fragmented, and the computer slows down. This is due to the fact that the computer needs to search multiple locations for fragments of a file, before it can open the file.

Disk Defragmenter is an auxiliary program that reorganizes the data on the hard drive and re-assembles the fragmented files, so the computer can operate more efficiently. In *Windows Vista* and *Windows 7* you can let *Disk Defragmenter* operate on a regular schedule, so you will not have to check whether the computer needs to be defragmented. But if you wish, you can also execute *Disk Defragmenter* manually. See more information about automatic defragmentation in the *Tip section 2.7 Defragmenting Your Computer in Windows 7* or *2.8 Defragmenting Your Computer in Windows Vista*.

The defragmentation process using *Disk Defragmenter* may take just a few minutes, but may also take up to several hours, depending on the size of the hard drive, the degree of fragmentation, and the amount of free space on the computer. To defragment, you will need at least 15% free space available. If there is not enough free space, you will need to delete some files first, or move them to other drives.

During the defragmentation process you can keep using your computer.

Do you have multiple drives or partitions? You can defragment these drives or partitions separately. The drive which contains the largest number of modifications, usually the drive containing your data files, will often be the most fragmented.

Source: Windows Help and Support

2.15 Tips

💡 Tip

Change the AutoComplete settings
In *Internet Explorer* you can determine whether web addresses, forms or passwords are to be completed automatically when you start typing in the address bar or in a form field. This can be useful if you do not want other users to see which websites you have visited.

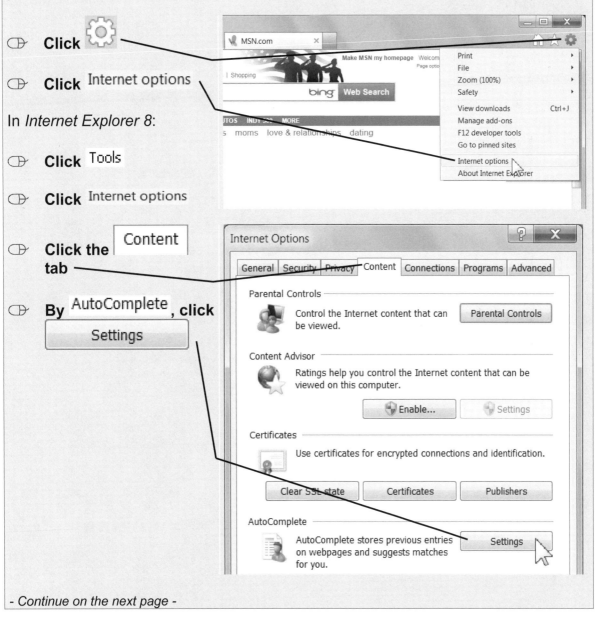

Click ⚙

Click Internet options

In *Internet Explorer 8*:

Click Tools

Click Internet options

Click the Content tab

By AutoComplete, click Settings

- Continue on the next page -

Now you will see a window where you can use check boxes 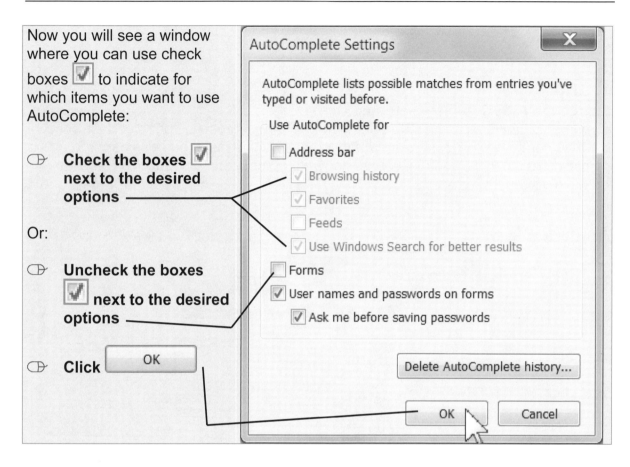 to indicate for which items you want to use AutoComplete:

☞ **Check the boxes** ✓
next to the desired options ─────────

Or:

☞ **Uncheck the boxes**
✓ **next to the desired options** ─────────

☞ **Click** [OK]

3. Keeping Your Computer Up-To-Date

Windows is continually being adjusted, improved, and secured even more. The additions and improvements are distributed by *Microsoft* by way of *software updates*. These updates can be downloaded automatically from the Internet by *Windows*. The *Windows Update* program takes care of this. This program will check whether you are using the most recent *Windows* version.

When you turn your computer on, the *Windows* program will start up, along with several other programs. Some of these programs are important, such as an antivirus program. But there can also be other programs that start up automatically, such as *Internet Explorer*, an instant messaging service or a calendar. During installation, these programs have been added to the list of *autorun* programs, or you may have added them manually yourself. These programs slow down the computer's startup process and also cause the computer to function more slowly. In this chapter you can read how to manage these autorun programs.

The speed of your computer is determined by the components of which the computer consists. Programs always require a certain minimum performance from these components, in order to function properly. In *Windows* you can view the components in your computer as well as their performance. You can use this information to upgrade your computer (if you wish), by adding higher quality components or replacing older ones.

In this chapter you will learn how to:

- use *Windows Update*;
- manage autorun programs;
- find information about your system;
- view the performance/experience index.

Please note:

To perform the actions described in this chapter, you will need to use the administrator's account (be logged in as administrator). If you cannot use this account, you will not be able to change several settings. When this happens, *Windows* will display a warning message. In such a case you can just read through the relevant section.

3.1 Using Windows Update in Windows 7 and Vista

Windows Update is an important element of *Windows*. This program checks for new *Windows* updates.

➤ Please note:

Microsoft will never send software updates by e-mail. If you ever receive an e-mail with an attachment claiming to contain *Microsoft* software or a *Windows* update, you should never open this attachment. Immediately delete the e-mail message and do not forget to remove the e-mail from the *Deleted Items* folder as well.
These types of e-mails are sent by unscrupulous people who try to install unwanted or harmful software onto your computer.

If you want to be sure that you are using the most current *Windows* version, you need to enable *Automatic updates*:

☞ **Click**

☞ **Click** System and Security **or** System and Maintenance

☞ **Click** Windows Update

You will see the *Windows Update* window:

In this example you will see one update waiting to be installed:

To install this update right away:

☞ **Click**

[🛡 Install updates]

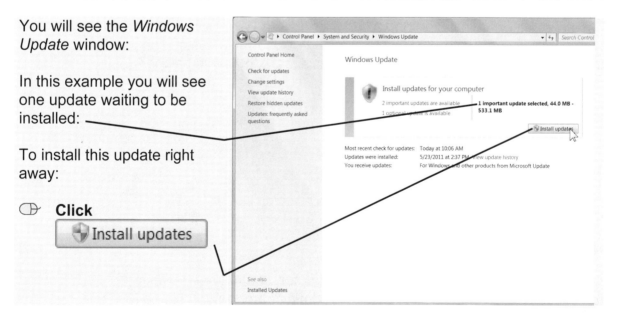

Usually, *Windows* will install new updates automatically when you turn your computer off.

By default, *Windows* is set to check for new updates automatically, but you can also perform this task manually:

If you let *Windows* search for new updates:

☞ **Click** Check for updates

You will see *Windows* checking for new updates:

If any new updates are found, you will see them in this window:

You can install these updates right away by clicking Install updates :

You can also view the settings for *Windows Update*:

☞ **Click** Change settings

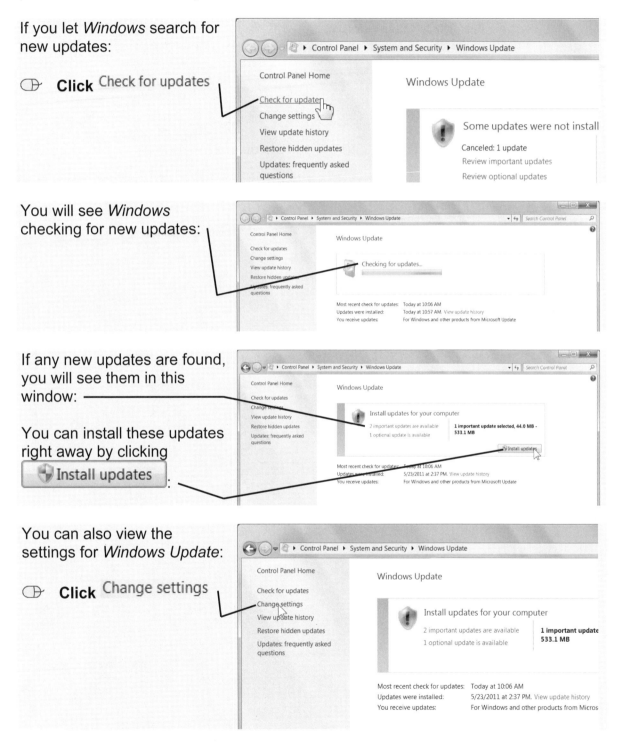

In this example, *Automatic updates* will check for new updates every day (night), at 3 AM. If the computer is not turned on at that moment, the program will check for new updates the next time you start it up. The available updates will be downloaded automatically and then installed. *Windows* may display a message about this on your desktop, but usually you can just carry on working. Important updates may require you to restart the computer.

It is recommended to select the

Install updates automatically (recommended) ▼

option. You can change the time to one that is convenient for you.

If the automatic update function is not enabled on your computer:

☞ **By** Important updates, **select** Install updates automatically

☞ **Click** 🛡 OK

If you have not changed anything:

☞ **Click** Cancel

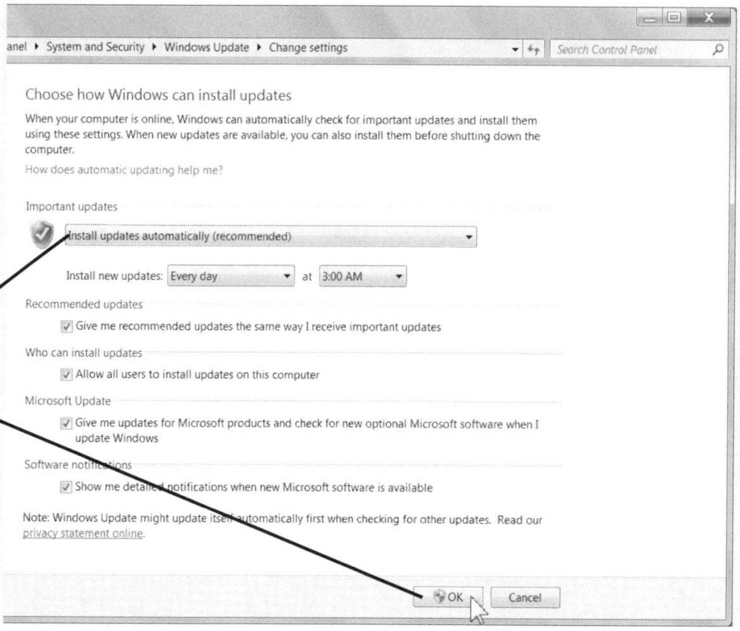

☞ **Close the *Windows Update* window** 👣²

3.2 Using Windows Update in Windows XP

Windows Update is an important element of *Windows XP*. This program checks for new *Windows* updates.

 Let op!

Microsoft will never send software updates by e-mail. If you ever receive an e-mail with an attachment claiming to contain *Microsoft* software or a *Windows* update, you should never open this attachment. Immediately delete the e-mail message and do not forget to remove the e-mail from the *Deleted Items* folder as well.
These types of e-mails are sent by unscrupulous people who try to install unwanted or harmful software onto your computer.

If you want to be sure you are using the most current version of *Windows XP*, you need to enable *Automatic updates*:

☞ **Click** start , Control Panel

☞ **Click** Security Center

☞ **Click** Automatic Updates

You will see the *Automatic Updates* window:

In this example, the automatic update function is disabled:

This means that security updates and other enhancements for *Windows*, among other things, will not be installed.

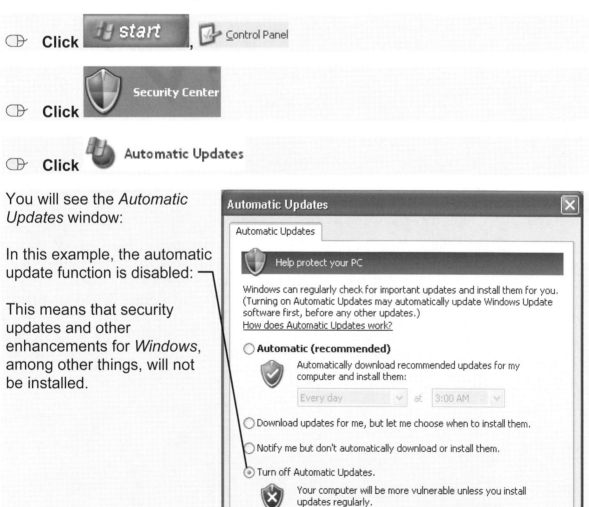

This is how you enable *Automatic Updates*:

☞ **Click the radio button ◉ by**
Automatic (recommended)

☞ **Click** [OK]

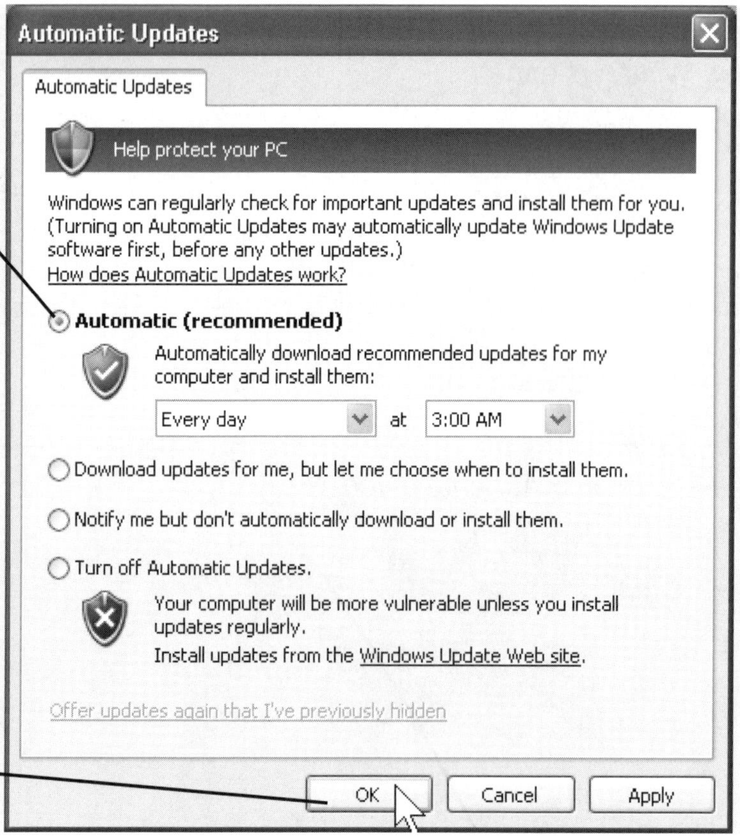

In this example, *Automatic Updates* will check for new updates every day (night), at 3 AM.

If the computer is not turned on at that moment, the program will check for new updates when you start it up. The available updates will be downloaded automatically and then installed. *Windows* may display a message about this on your desktop, but usually you can just carry on working. Important updates may require you to restart the computer.

☞ **Close all windows** ⚘²

3.3 Managing Autorun Programs

When you turn your computer on, a number of programs will startup automatically, along with *Windows*. These *autorun* programs can slow down your computer's startup process. They can also cause the computer in general to perform slower, because they are still running in the background and take up memory. Some programs are very useful when they are automatically started, such as antivirus programs. But other programs can be disabled from the automatic startup.
In *Windows Vista* and *Windows XP* you can open *Windows Defender* to view a list of all the programs that are started up automatically. You can delete certain programs from the list, if you wish. In *Windows 7*, this option has been replaced by a separate program which enables you to view all the details of the programs that are started up automatically. This program is called *Autoruns*. It can also be used in *Windows Vista* and *Windows XP*.

💡 Tip

Use Windows Defender in Windows Vista and XP
If you prefer using *Windows Defender* in *Windows Vista* or *XP*, you can take a look at our free booklet called *Windows Defender Guide*. You can find this PDF file on our web page **www.visualsteps.com/info_downloads.php**

You can download the *Autoruns* program for free from the *Microsoft* website:

👉 **Open** *Internet Explorer* ✂️¹

⌨️ **In the address bar, type:**
`technet.microsoft.com`

⌨️ **Press** `Enter ←`

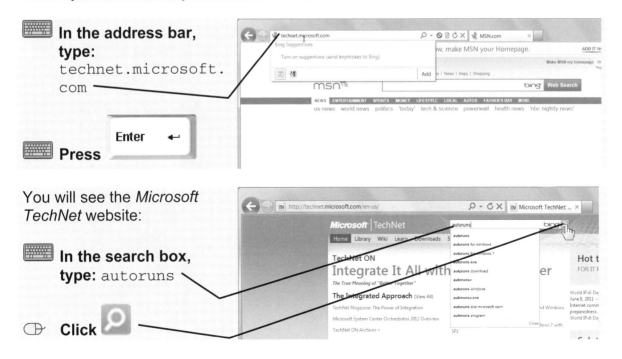

You will see the *Microsoft TechNet* website:

⌨️ **In the search box, type:** `autoruns`

👆 **Click** 🔍

You will see the search
results:

⊂⊃ **Click**
   Autoruns for Windows

Now you will see the
Autoruns web page:

You can start the program
directly from the website:

⊂⊃ **Click**
   Run Autoruns

In *Internet Explorer 9*:

⊂⊃ **Click** [Run]

In *Internet Explorer 8*:

⊂⊃ **Click** [Run]

In *Internet Explorer 8*:

⊂⊃ **Click** [Run]

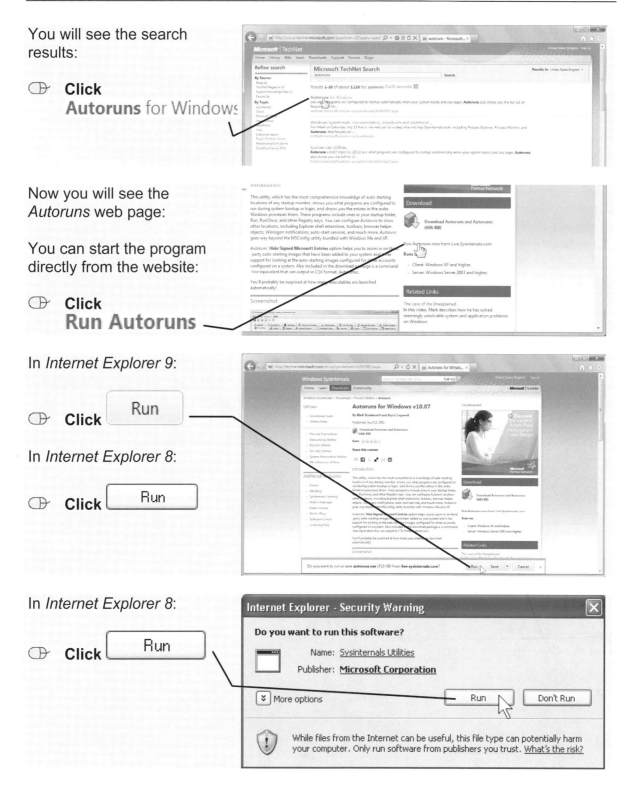

You will see this window:

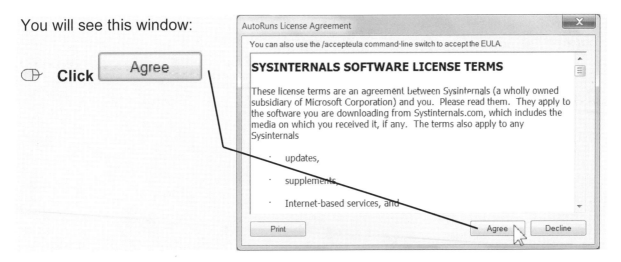

◯➔ **Click** [Agree]

Now the program will be started and your computer will be scanned:

You will see the *Autoruns* window:

All the autorun programs will be displayed:

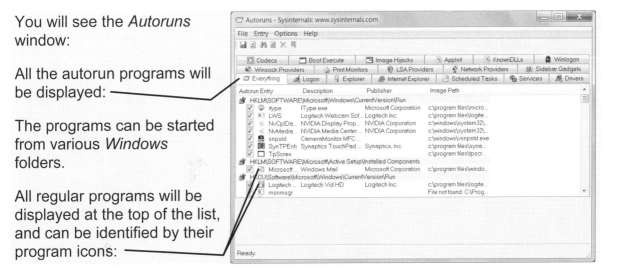

The programs can be started from various *Windows* folders.

All regular programs will be displayed at the top of the list, and can be identified by their program icons:

You can prevent a program from starting up automatically by disabling it. This will not permanently remove the program from the autorun folders, but it does make sure that the program does not run automatically.

🐾 Please note:

Disabling antivirus programs, drivers and communication programs in the autorun folders, may result in your computer malfunctioning. You should only disable the programs that you are familiar with. If any problems occur, you can always re-enable the program again by checking the box ☑ next to the program.

To disable an autorun
program:

⊕ **Uncheck the box** ☑
   next to the program

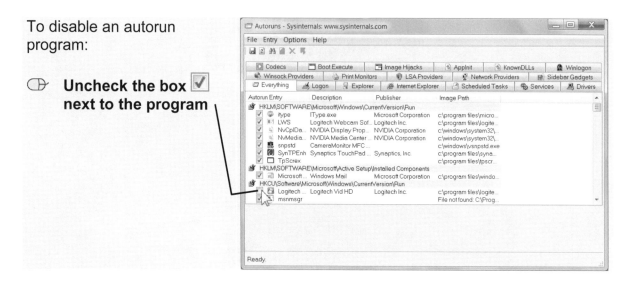

🩹 **HELP! I see a different window**

When you are trying to disable specific categories, you may see the *Autoruns Access Denied* window. This is how you can still disable the autorun program:

⊕ **Click**

[🛡 Run as Administrator]

Autoruns Access Denied   ✕

⚠ Error changing item state: Toegang geweigerd.

[🛡 Run as Administrator]   [Cancel]

⊕ **Click the *Autoruns* taskbar button**

⊕ **Uncheck the box** ☑ **next to the program**

☞ **Close all windows** 👣²

3.4 Basic Information about the Windows 7 and Vista Systems

Your computer's performance is determined by many different factors. Important components are the *processor* and the *internal memory*, also called the *working memory* or *RAM* (*Random Access Memory*). This is how to view these components:

☞ **Click** , Control Panel

☞ **Click** System and Security **or** System and Maintenance

☞ **Click** System

Now you will see basic information about your computer.

The *Windows* version and possible installed *Service Packs*: ———————

System and Security ▸ System	▾ ↵ Search Control Panel 🔍

View basic information about your computer

Windows edition

Windows 7 Ultimate
Copyright © 2009 Microsoft Corporation. All rights reserved.

Once *Windows* has been installed on your computer, adjustments and enhancements, developed by *Microsoft*, will be installed as well. These are the so-called *updates*. These updates will be installed automatically when you connect to the Internet, provided you have enabled the automatic updates function. Major adaptations of the software are called *Service Packs*.

The speed rating: ——————

You can read more about this in *section 3.7 Viewing the Experience Index in Windows 7 and Vista.*

The processor brand and type: ——————

System

Rating:	4.4 Windows Experience Index
Processor:	Intel(R) Core(TM)2 CPU T5500 @ 1.66GHz 1.67 GHz
Installed memory (RAM):	2.00 GB
System type:	32-bit Operating System
Pen and Touch:	No Pen or Touch Input is available for this Display

Computer name, domain, and workgroup settings

Computer name:	Visual7	Change settings
Full computer name:	Visual7	
Computer description:		
Workgroup:	WORKGROUP	

Windows activation

You must activate today. Activate Windows now

The processor is the core of your computer. All operations on the computer are directed through the processor. Modern processors compute at a very fast speed: millions of operations per second.

This processor speed is expressed in *megahertz* (MHz) or *gigahertz* (GHz). The higher the number, the faster the processor will be, and therefore, the computer too.

The RAM memory:

The RAM memory of the computer is the internal memory or working memory. *Windows*, as well as all the programs you use and the documents you are editing, are stored in the RAM memory while you are working. This memory is much faster than the hard disk. Before you turn your computer off or restart it, you will need to save your work first, because the RAM memory can only remember data as long as the computer is turned on. The size of the RAM memory is expressed in *megabytes* (MB) or *gigabytes* (GB).

Tip

Work faster with a larger RAM memory
If you have a larger RAM memory, the data that is in use while you are working will not have to be retrieved as often from the slower hard drive. This will speed up your computer while you are working. Expanding your RAM memory is an inexpensive and easy method of speeding up your computer.

In *Windows 7* and *Vista* you will see a 32 bits or 64 bits operating system next to *System type:*.

You can read more about the different operating systems in the *Background Information* at the end of this chapter.

Here you will see your computer name: ————

By *Computer description:* you will see the name that is displayed to other users of your computer or in your network: ————

System	
Rating:	Windows Experience Index
Processor:	Intel(R) Core(TM)2 CPU T5500 @ 1.66GHz 1.67 GHz
Installed memory (RAM):	2.00 GB
System type:	32-bit Operating System
Pen and Touch:	No Pen or Touch Input is available for this Display

Computer name, domain, and workgroup settings

Computer name:	Visual7	Change settings
Full computer name:	Visual7	
Computer description:		
Workgroup:	WORKGROUP	

Windows activation

You must activate today. Activate Windows now

Here you can see whether your *Windows* version has been activated by *Microsoft*:

A non-activated version cannot be fully used.

You will also see the Product ID: ————

System	
Rating:	Windows Experience Index
Processor:	Intel(R) Core(TM)2 CPU T5500 @ 1.66GHz 1.67 GHz
Installed memory (RAM):	2.00 GB
System type:	32-bit Operating System
Pen and Touch:	No Pen or Touch Input is available for this Display

Computer name, domain, and workgroup settings

Computer name:	Visual7	Change settings
Full computer name:	Visual7	
Computer description:		
Workgroup:	WORKGROUP	

Windows activation

Product-id: 00426-292-6137731-85917

☞ **Close the *System* window** 🐾*2*

🔖 **Please note:**

> Never change the Product ID! A different Product ID will need to be activated all over again. If you do not have the correct activation code, *Windows* will not function anymore.

3.5 Basic Information about the Windows XP System

Your computer's performance is determined by many different factors. Important components are the *processor* and the *internal memory*, also called the *working memory* or *RAM* (*Random Access Memory*). This is how to view these components:

☞ **Click** ▮ *start* , 🗹 Control Panel

☞ **Click** 🥧 **Performance and Maintenance**

☞ **Click** 🖥 System

You will see basic information about your computer.

The *Windows XP* version, and any possible installed *Service Packs*:

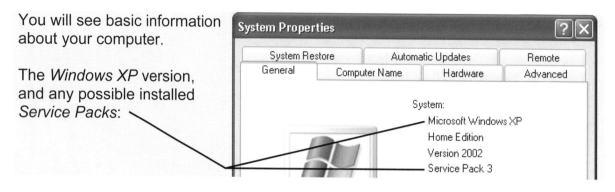

Once *Windows* has been installed on your computer, adjustments and enhancements, developed by *Microsoft*, will be installed as well. These are the so-called *updates*. These updates will be installed automatically when you connect to the Internet, provided you have enabled the automatic updates function. Major adaptations of the software are called *Service Packs*.

The processor brand and type:

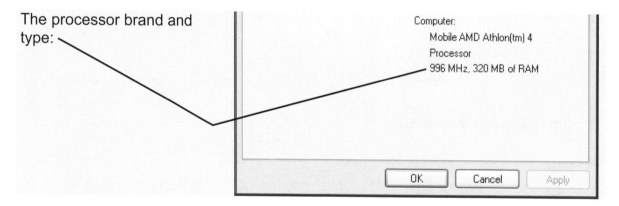

The processor is the core of your computer. All operations on the computer are directed through the processor. Modern processors compute at a very fast speed: millions of operations per second. This processor speed is expressed in *megahertz* (MHz) or *gigahertz* (GHz). The higher the number, the faster the processor will be, and therefore, the computer too.

The RAM memory:

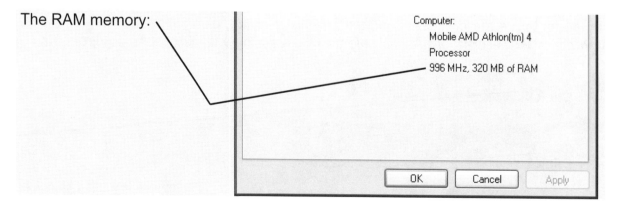

The RAM memory of the computer is the internal memory, or working memory. *Windows*, as well as the programs you use and the documents you are editing, are stored in the RAM memory while you are working. This memory is much faster than the hard drive. Before you turn your computer off or restart it, you will need to save your work first, because the RAM memory can only remember data as long as the computer is turned on. The size of the RAM memory is expressed in *megabytes* (MB) or *gigabytes* (GB).

Tip

Work faster with a larger RAM memory
If you have a larger RAM memory, the data that is in use while you are working will not have to be retrieved as often from the slower hard drive. This will speed up your computer while you are working. Expanding your RAM memory is an inexpensive and easy method of speeding up your computer.

Here you can see if your *Windows* version has been registered by *Microsoft*:

A non-registered version cannot be fully used.

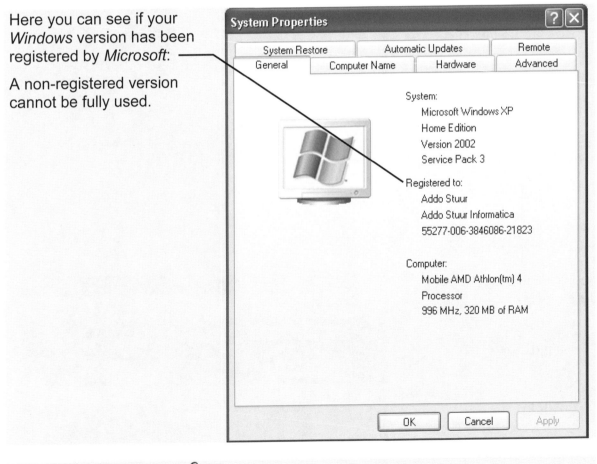

☞ **Close all windows** 📏²

3.6 System Information

A computer consists of a large number of components. In the *System Information* window you will see an overview of your entire computer system. This is how to open the *System Information* window:

In *Windows 7* and *Vista*:

Click

In the search box, type: system information

Click System Information

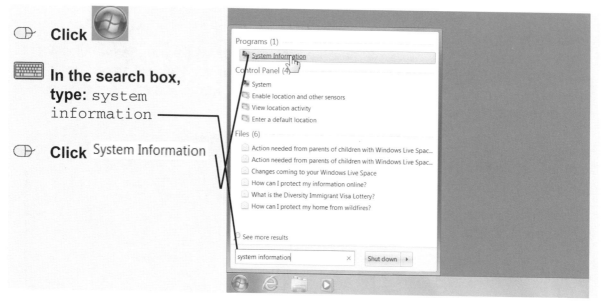

In *Windows XP*:

Click start , Help and Support

You will see the *Help and Support Center*:

Click Support

Click Advanced System Information

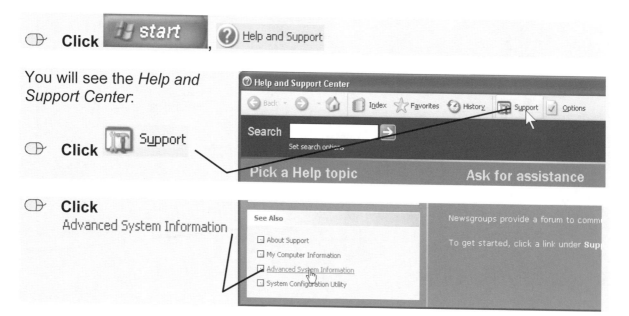

⊕ **Click**
  View detailed system inform

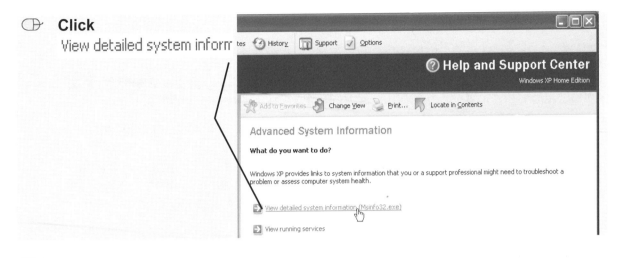

Please note:

In the following screen shots you will see a number of windows containing a lot of technical information. Most of this information will make sense to technicians, but not to the average computer user. Feel free to take a look at the information, but do not worry if you cannot fully understand it. Nevertheless, it can be useful to know where you can find this kind of information, for instance, if you need to provide information about your system to the technicians at a helpdesk.

You will see extensive information about your computer:

⊕ **By** Hardware Resources **,**
  click ⊞

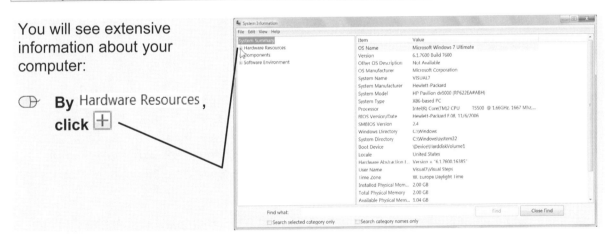

The System Information window

The *System Information* window shows details about your computer's hardware configuration, computer components and software, including drivers.

System Information lists categories in the left pane and details about each category in the right pane. The categories include:

- *System Summary*: Displays general information about your computer and the operating system, such as the computer name and manufacturer, the type of basic input/output system (BIOS) your computer uses and the amount of memory that is installed.
- *Hardware Resources*: Displays advanced details about your computer's hardware and is intended for IT professionals.
- *Components*: Displays information about disk drives, sound devices, modems and other components installed on your computer.
- *Software Environment*: Displays information about drivers, network connections and other program-related details.

To find a specific detail in *System Information*, type the information you are looking for in the *Find what* box at the bottom of the window. For example, to find your computer's Internet protocol (IP) address, type IP address in the Find what: box, and then click Find .

Source: Windows Help and Support

For example, just take a look at the *IRQ's* (*Interrupt Request*). These are the alarms with which a device can demand attention from the processor. It could be a printer that indicates that the paper tray is empty, for instance. It is important that two similar devices do not use the same IRQ, because the processor will not know which device will need the attention. This may lead to malfunctioning devices. This is how you can view the IRQ's:

☞ **Click** IRQ's

You will see all the IRQ's, and the devices that use them:

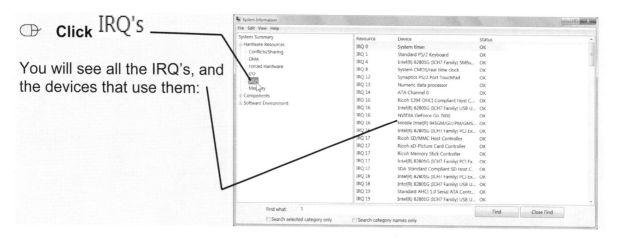

Normally, IRQ's are set when the device is installed. Do not change IRQ's, unless the device is not functioning properly.

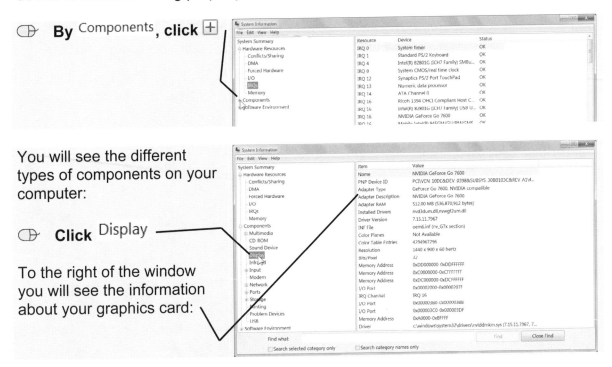

⊕ **By** Components **, click** ⊞

You will see the different types of components on your computer:

⊕ **Click** Display

To the right of the window you will see the information about your graphics card:

💡 **Tip**

Solving problems
Are you experiencing problems with a specific device? Then click Problem Devices , by Components . You will see if the device has a problem with *Windows* or if you need to search for a solution in a different direction.

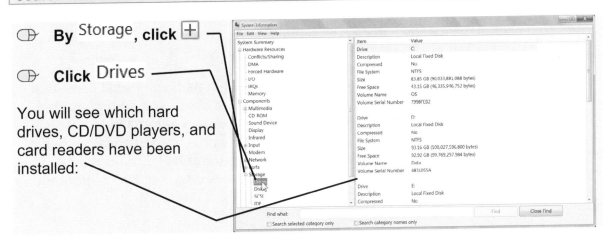

⊕ **By** Storage **, click** ⊞

⊕ **Click** Drives

You will see which hard drives, CD/DVD players, and card readers have been installed:

For each storage device, there is information about the type of drive or card and which letter designates the device on the file system for which the device is formatted.

In this window you can also view information about the software programs that are installed:

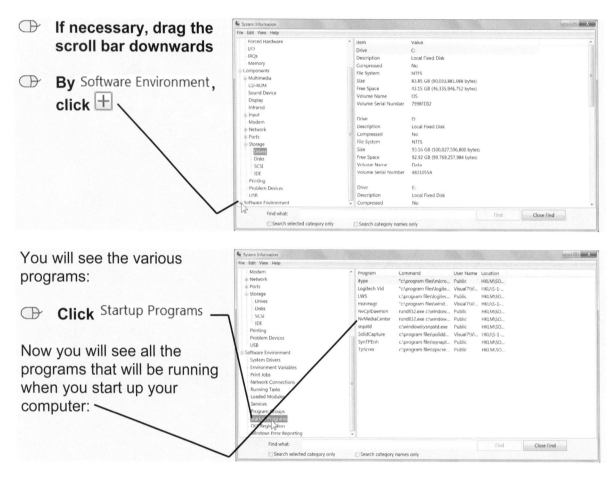

☞ **If necessary, drag the scroll bar downwards**

☞ **By** Software Environment, **click** ⊞

You will see the various programs:

☞ **Click** Startup Programs

Now you will see all the programs that will be running when you start up your computer:

You may not recognize some of the program names. Such as background tasks that take care of directing your mouse or a webcam. However, if you see some familiar program names, you can decide whether or not to run these programs automatically at startup. By preventing some of these programs from starting automatically, your computer may run a bit faster. In *section 3.3 Managing Autorun Programs* we have explained how to do this. Important programs listed here are your antivirus program and your firewall. Be sure not to disable these programs.

Please note:

If you click Windows Error Reporting, you will get an overview of the *Windows* system errors and errors from the programs you have used. Generating this list may take a long time and the information is on the technical side. Meanwhile you will see the message **Refreshing System Information...** .

An example of *Windows Error Reporting*:

Close all windows $\partial\!\!\!\!\!\partial^{2}$

3.7 Viewing the Experience Index in Windows 7 and Vista

The way in which you use your computer can make a lot of difference with respect to its performance. If you play a lot of 3D games or use the computer for editing videos, the demands on the system will be much higher than when you just use the computer for sending e-mails. The *Windows Performance Index* (*Windows Experience Index*) will give you a clue about the suitability of your computer for doing specific tasks.

Please note:

Windows XP does not contain a tool for monitoring the performance index.

This is how to view the *Windows Experience Index*:

Click

In the search box, **type:** performance

Click Performance Information

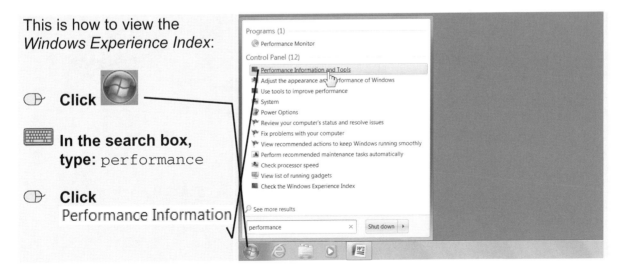

You will see your computer's score. This ranges from 1.0 (slow) to 7.9 (fast) in *Windows 7* and from 1.0 to 5.9 in *Windows Vista*:

The score will be computed for the current situation; if anything in your computer changes, the score will need to be computed again.

👉 **Click** Re-run the assessment

   or 🛡️ Rate this computer

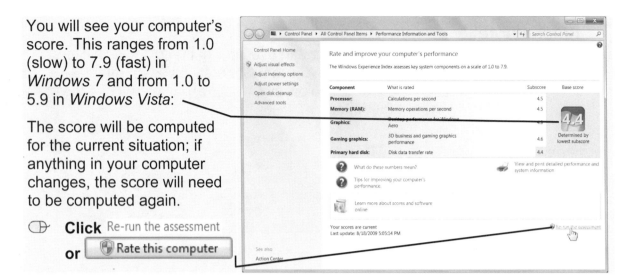

📧 **If necessary, give permission to continue**

While the score is being assessed, you will see this window:

> **Windows Experience Index**   ✖
>
> ### Running the Direct3D 9 Aero Assessment
>
> This might take a few minutes. Your screen might flash during the rating.

You will see the new score:

The score will correspond with the lowest score from a specific component. In this case, it is the hard disk speed:

Rate and improve your computer's performance

The Windows Experience Index assesses key system components on a scale of 1.0 to 7.9.

Component	What is rated	Subscore	Base score
Processor:	Calculations per second	4.5	
Memory (RAM):	Memory operations per second	4.5	
Graphics:	Desktop performance for Windows Aero	4.9	4.4
Gaming graphics:	3D business and gaming graphics performance	4.6	Determined by lowest subscore
Primary hard disk:	Disk data transfer rate	4.4	

❓ What do these numbers mean?

❓ Tips for improving your computer's performance.

🖨️ View and print detailed performance and system information

You can find more information about the base scores in *section 3.8 Background Information*.

📧 **Close the window** 👣²

3.8 Visual Steps Website and Newsletter

So you have noticed that the Visual Steps-method is a great method to gather knowledge quickly and efficiently. All the books published by Visual Steps have been written according to this method. There are quite a lot of books available, on different subjects. For instance about *Windows*, photo editing, and about free programs, such as *Google Earth* and *Skype*.

Book + software
One of the Visual Steps books includes a CD with the program that is discussed. The full version of this high quality, easy-to-use software is included. You can recognize this Visual Steps book with enclosed CD by this logo on the book cover:

Website
Use the blue *Catalog* button on the **www.visualsteps.com** website to read an extensive description of all available Visual Steps titles, including the full table of contents and part of a chapter (as a PDF file). In this way you can find out if the book is what you expected.

This instructive website also contains:
- free computer booklets and informative guides (PDF files) on a range of subjects;
- free computer tips, described according to the Visual Steps method;
- a large number of frequently asked questions and their answers;
- information on the free Computer certificate you can obtain on the online test website **www.ccforseniors.com**;
- free 'Notify me' e-mail service: receive an e-mail when book of interest are published.

Visual Steps Newsletter
Do you want to keep yourself informed of all Visual Steps publications? Then subscribe (no strings attached) to the free Visual Steps Newsletter, which is sent by e-mail.

This Newsletter is issued once a month and provides you with information on:
- the latest titles, as well as older books;
- special offers and discounts;
- new, free computer booklets and guides.

As a subscriber to the Visual Steps Newsletter you have direct access to the free booklets and guides, at **www.visualsteps.com/info_downloads**

3.9 Background Information

Dictionary	
Autorun program	A program that runs automatically when you startup *Windows*.
Autoruns	A program that shows you the details of all the programs that start automatically in *Windows*. You can download or open this program for free, from the *Microsoft* website.
Base score	The base score indicates the overall performance of your system, based on the capacity of the various components of your computer. A higher base score usually means that the computer will perform better and faster than a computer with a lower base score, especially when you need to execute complicated tasks such as video editing.
Performance index	The performance (experience) index measures the capacity of the hardware and software configuration of your computer and expresses the results as a figure that is called the base score.
Processor	The most important chip in a computer. The processor (or CPU) executes the majority of the computations necessary to make the computer perform.
RAM memory	The main internal memory storage area used by the computer for executing programs and storing data. Data will be temporarily stored in the RAM memory and will be lost when you turn the computer off. The RAM memory is also called the internal memory or the working memory.
Service Pack	A software update which contains new security functions and enhancements, combined with existing updates. Contrary to regular updates, *Service Packs* can contain new functions or changes in the software design of a specific product.
System information	This tool contains advanced, detailed information for technicians, about the configuration, components and software, such as drivers.
Windows Update	A program that checks if you are using the most current version of the *Windows* operating system.

Source: Windows Help and Support

What does the base score mean?

The base score (only available in *Windows 7* and *Vista*) represents the overall performance of your system, based on the capabilities of different parts of your computer, including random access memory (RAM), central processing unit (CPU), hard drive, general graphics performance on the desktop and 3-D graphics capability.

Here are general descriptions of the experience you can expect from a computer that receives the following base scores:

- A computer with a base score of 2.0 usually has sufficient performance to do general computing tasks, such as run business programs and search the Internet. However, a computer with this base score is generally not powerful enough to run *Windows Aero*, or the advanced multimedia experiences that are available with *Windows 7*.
- A computer with a base score of 3.0 can run *Windows Aero* and many features of *Windows* at a basic level. Some of the *Windows* advanced features might not have all of their functionality available. For example, a computer with a base score of 3.0 can display the *Windows* theme at a resolution of 1280 × 1024, but might struggle to run the theme on multiple monitors. Another example: this computer can play digital TV content but might struggle to play high-definition television (HDTV) content.
- In *Windows Vista*, a computer with a base score of 4.0 or 5.0 can run all new *Windows* functions with their full functionality. The computer will support advanced, graphics-intensive applications such as multi-player 3D games, and recording or playing HDTV content. When *Windows* was released, computers with a base score of 5.0 were the top-performing computers available at the time.
- A computer with a base score of 4.0 or 5.0 can run new features of *Windows 7* and it can run multiple programs at the same time.
- A computer with a base score of 6.0 or 7.0 has a faster hard drive and can support high-end, graphics-intensive experiences such as multiplayer and 3-D gaming and recording and playback of HDTV content.

- Continue on the next page -

The *Windows Experience Index* is designed to accommodate advances in computer technology. As hardware speed and performance improve, higher score ranges will be enabled. The standards for each level of the index generally stay the same. This means the base score of a computer also stays the same, unless you decide to upgrade the hardware. For instance, if you need a higher score than your current base score to run a specific program in *Windows*.

If you have installed new hardware and you want to see if your score has changed, you need to click Re-run the assessment or ⬛ **Rate this computer**. If you want to display the computer's hardware details, then click
View and print detailed performance and system information .

Source: Windows Help and Support

Processor
The processor is the most critical component of your computer. All operations you execute on the computer are computed by the processor. Even when you are typing some text in a text editor or editing a photo, the processor will be busy computing these operations.
Modern processors compute at a lightning speed. The speed of the processor is measured in *megahertz* or *gigahertz,* for example *800 MHz* or *3 GHz*. The higher the number, the faster the processor works and the faster your computer will be.

In the end, the speed will also be determined by the speed of the other components in your computer. If the processor is fast but other components are not so fast, you may experience some sluggishness. You may notice that it seems to take more time to open a file or a program or save your work.

In the past few years, various manufacturers have developed a large number of processors. Well-known types were:
- *Intel 8088/8086/80286*:
  These processors were used in the first computers. They were able to process 8 to 16 bits at once, and that is why they were called 8 or 16 bits processors. A bit is a single computer signal, for instance on/off, yes/no, or 0 and 1. Computers can only work with bits.
- *Intel 80386/80486*:
  This processor worked with 32 bits at once and therefore it was faster and could handle larger amounts of data.

- Continue on the next page -

- *Intel Pentium/Celeron*:
  The most recent 32 bits processors are best suited for *Windows*. The *Pentium M* is a special version used by laptops ('M' stands for mobile), which is less power consuming.
  There also exist 64 bits versions of the Pentium processors. They are not as popular yet, because much of the software available today is still 32 bits. But this will surely change in the future.

Similar types of processors are made by other manufacturers such as AMD and Cyrix.

Modern processors are fitted as multi-core processors. These processors have multiple cores (dual-core, for example, has two cores), which work independently. This results in shorter waiting periods.
If you want to use these systems, the operating system and also all the programs will need to use the multi-core technology. *Windows* uses this technology along with many other modern programs.

Memory types
Apart from hard drives, CDs and DVDs, a computer also uses other types of electronic memory. Electronic memory is much faster than the mechanical memory of the types mentioned above.

RAM	*Random Access Memory* also called working memory or internal memory. The most important internal storage area that is used by the computer to execute programs and store data. Data will be temporarily stored in the RAM memory and will be lost when you turn off or restart the computer. The RAM memory consists of a number of (cards with) memory chips and can often be expanded by adding an extra card. Because these chips are very fast, the size of the RAM memory influences the speed at which you can work. Keep in mind that RAM memory comes in different types and speeds. A memory card with the wrong speed can result in technical troubles while you are working.
ROM	*Read Only Memory* or memory that can only be read. Built-in computer memory that can be read, but not modified by a computer. Contrary to RAM memory, the data in the ROM memory will not be erased when the computer is turned off. Among other things, the ROM memory contains all the necessary instructions for starting up the computer when it is turned on.

- Continue on the next page -

Flash	A small device used to store information, such as a USB stick. USB sticks can be connected to the computer's USB port. They allow you to copy and exchange data between different computers. The stored data will be saved in the memory, even after you have disconnected the stick from the USB port. The memory can be cleared and re-written. The memory cards in cameras and mobile phones also use flash memory.
Virtual	Temporary storage space on a disk or USB stick that is used by a computer to execute programs that require more RAM memory than is available in the computer.
Cache	Cache memory is a very fast but expensive type of memory that is built-in in a processor or hard drive. This memory is used for temporary storage of much-used data, so the computer will not need to look up this data every time. This memory is also used to store the index tables that are required for looking up data. A large cache memory can considerably enhance the computer speed. Because this type of memory is built-in in the processor or your hard drive, you cannot expand it yourself.

Out of all these types of memory, it is the RAM memory that influences the speed of the computer the most as you work. Keep in mind that the 32 bits version of *Windows* can directly process up to a maximum of 4 GB. If the RAM memory is larger than this, you will not gain a lot of speed.

Expanding the hardware to speed up your computer

Even if your settings are optimized for maximum speed, your computer's performance will eventually decline. Installing newer and faster hardware might still be a solution. Here are some ways of expanding your computer in an effective way:

Faster hard drive

A faster internal hard drive can enhance the speed a lot. Pay attention to the speed of the drive, usually expressed in rpm (rotations per minute). A drive with 5400 rpm is clearly slower than a drive with 7200 rpm. Also, you can buy hard drives which are equipped with a cache memory, a very fast type of memory. This memory will temporarily store much-used data, so it does not need to be retrieved from the (slower) hard drive each time you want to use it. Cache memory is not easily expanded, so choose a large cache memory if speed matters.

External hard drives will always experience some delay because of the data transfer through a USB or firewire connection. When you buy a new hard drive, also pay attention to the speed of this connection.

Extra RAM memory

RAM memory is inexpensive and greatly influences the speed. But keep in mind that the 32 bits version of *Windows* can directly handle up to a maximum of 4 GB. If the RAM memory is larger than this, you will not gain a lot of speed.

Faster graphics card

Windows and other programs increasingly use graphic functions. A faster graphics card will cause the windows to be displayed much faster and will take some of the pressure off the processor. A graphics card that uses *shared memory* (part of your RAM memory), is notably slower than a card that has its own graphic memory.

Faster processor

This seems to be the most obvious solution, but it is relatively expensive and the effect will also depend on the rest of your computer's components. Also, not every motherboard is suited to a faster processor.

Which method of expanding your computer is most effective, will mainly depend on the way you use your computer. If you try to become aware of exactly what point your computer starts to slow down, you may be able to determine which component causes the delay.

Notes

Appendix A How Do I Do That Again?

In this book actions are marked with footsteps: 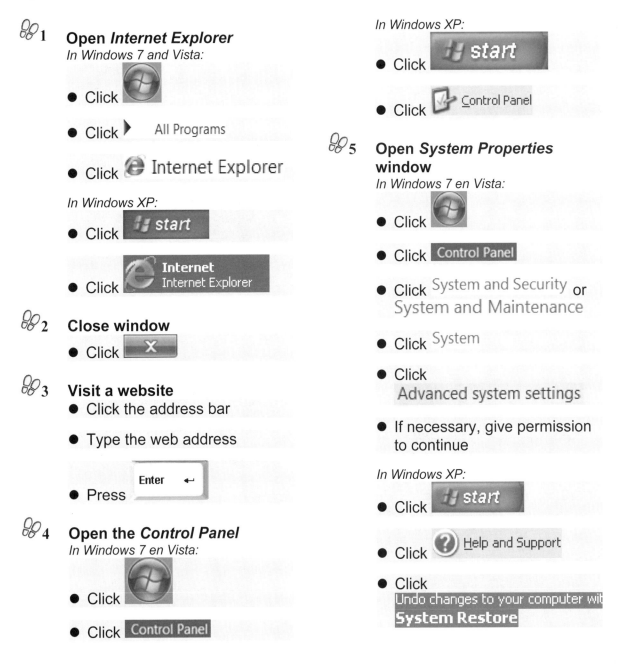1
Find the corresponding number in the appendix below to see how to execute a specific operation.

1 **Open *Internet Explorer***
In Windows 7 and Vista:

- Click

- Click ▶ All Programs

- Click 🅮 Internet Explorer

In Windows XP:

- Click **start**

- Click **Internet** Internet Explorer

2 **Close window**
- Click X

3 **Visit a website**
- Click the address bar

- Type the web address

- Press Enter ↵

4 **Open the *Control Panel***
In Windows 7 en Vista:

- Click

- Click Control Panel

In Windows XP:

- Click **start**

- Click Control Panel

5 **Open *System Properties* window**
In Windows 7 en Vista:

- Click

- Click Control Panel

- Click System and Security or System and Maintenance

- Click System

- Click Advanced system settings

- If necessary, give permission to continue

In Windows XP:

- Click **start**

- Click ⍰ Help and Support

- Click Undo changes to your computer wit **System Restore**

Appendix B Replacing the Antivirus Program

If you want to install *Microsoft Security Essentials*, it is best to remove any other antivirus program that was previously installed. Before you do this, however, make sure that you have already downloaded and saved the *Microsoft Security Essentials* installation file. Next, you can delete the old program and continue installing *Microsoft Security Essentials*. In the following steps we will explain how you do this.

☞ **Open *Internet Explorer* ℗¹**

☞ **Open the www.microsoft.com/securityessentials website ℗³**

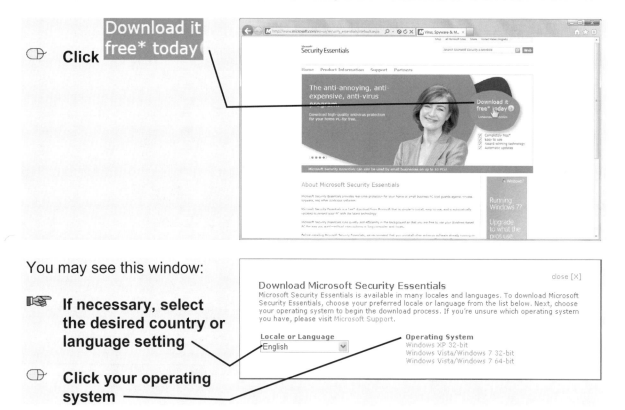

⊕ **Click**

You may see this window:

☞ **If necessary, select the desired country or language setting**

⊕ **Click your operating system**

You can save the file:

In *Internet Explorer 9*:

☞ **By** [Save] **, click** [▾]

☞ **Click** Save as

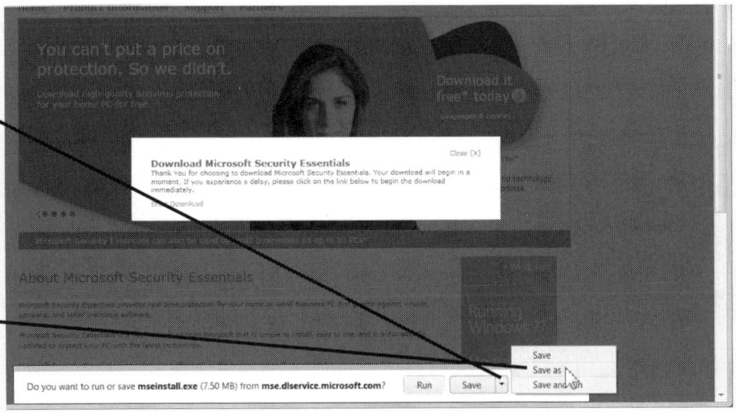

In *Internet Explorer 8*:

☞ **Click** [Save]

You are going to save the file to your desktop:

☞ **Click** Desktop

☞ **Click** [Save]

The file will be saved.

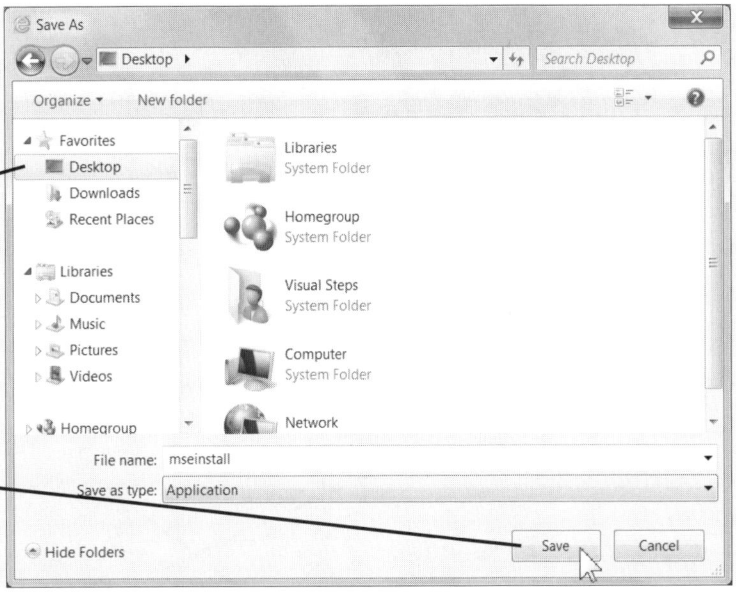

To make sure that your computer is not threatened after you have removed the antivirus program, it is best to temporary disable the Internet connection.

☞ **Disconnect the network cable from the computer, or disable the wireless network connection**

Now you can delete the old antivirus program.

☞ **Close all windows** 🐾²

In this example we will be deleting the *Adobe Reader* program. Of course, at home you will want to select and remove your old antivirus program.

☞ **Open the *Control Panel* ⚙⁴**

You will see the *Control Panel*:

☞ **By** Programs **, click** Uninstall a program

In *Windows XP*:

☞ **Click**

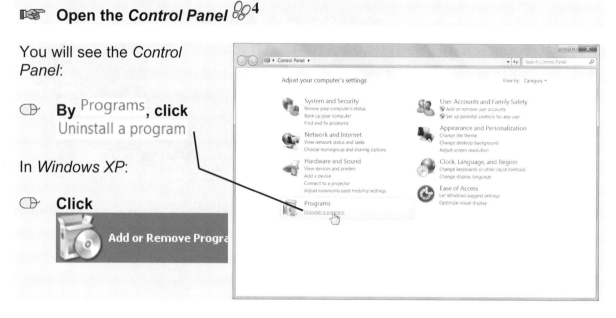

You will see a list with all the programs you might possibly remove. You are going to select your antivirus program.

First you select the program.

☞ **Click the antivirus program**

Next, you can remove the program.

☞ **Click** Uninstall

In *Windows XP* the Remove button can be found next to the program.

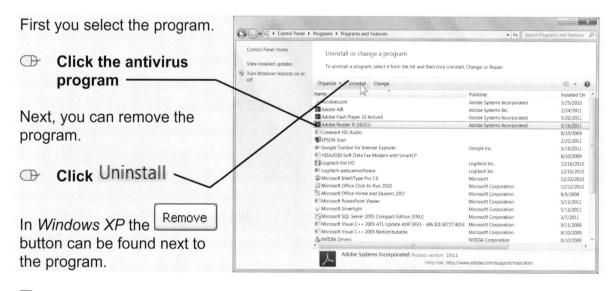

➤ **Please note:**

The windows that will now appear may be different from the examples in this book. This depends on the antivirus program you want to remove. You may also need to restart your computer as well.

Windows will ask you if you
are sure you want to remove
this program:

Programs and Features
⚠ Are you sure you want to uninstall Adobe Reader X (10.0.1)?
☐ In the future, do not show me this dialog box   [Yes]   [No]

☞ **Click** [**Yes**]

Now the program will be removed from the computer.

➥ **Please note:**

When you are uninstalling a program, some programs will ask you if you just want to
uninstall some of the program's components, and you may see additional windows.

☞ **Follow the operations in the windows**

☞ **Close all windows** ²

☞ **Restart the computer**

Now the old antivirus program has been removed. You can now proceed with the
installation of *Microsoft Security Essentials*.

On your desktop, you should see the following icon:

☞ **Double-click**

If you are using a *Windows 7* or *Windows Vista* computer, your screen will turn dark
when the installation process begins. *Windows* will then ask for your permission to
continue:

☞ **Click** [Allow] **or** [Yes]

To fully install the program:

☞ **Continue on page 30 in this book**

After you have followed all the steps, you can delete the installation file that was saved earlier. This is how you do that:

On the desktop:

☞ **Right-click**

You will see a menu:

☞ **Click** Delete

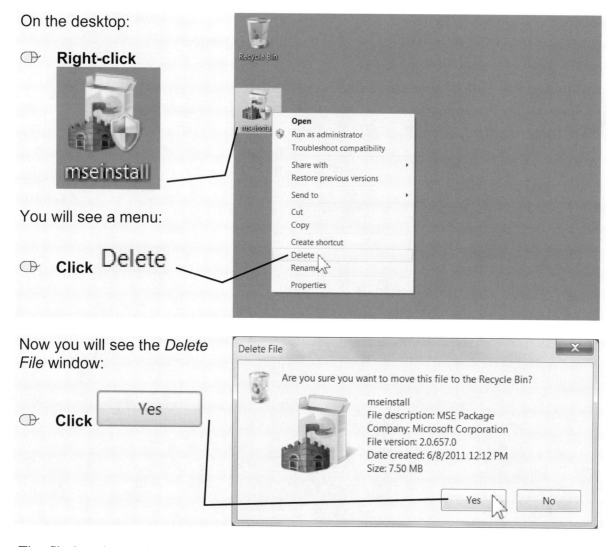

Now you will see the *Delete File* window:

☞ **Click** Yes

The file has been deleted. Now you can restore the Internet connection:

☞ **Connect the network cable to the computer or enable the wireless network connection**

Appendix C Index